Endorsements

"I am so blessed by Dr. Maureen Anderson's new book, GOD'S GRACE FUELS MY PASSION. Wow, what a statement! I really enjoyed this book and believe that you will, too. It's a total and complete understanding of what grace is, what grace does, and what grace will do.
Get ready to fuel your passion with God's amazing grace!"

- Jesse Duplantis

"I love how Dr. Maureen Anderson profoundly unveils the powerful, life-changing message of the grace of God. After reading this book, you'll walk away knowing you are loved, forgiven, qualified, justified and covered in God's amazing grace."

- April Osteen Simon

"Jeanne and I have known Maureen for many years. She is the consummate example of a lady of faith and power.
Maureen is an excellent teacher of the Word of God. She not only knows what the Word says, but she has applied godly principles to her own life and ministry. Through revelation and experience, she is teaching and inspiring others to rise up and become winners.
I know this new book, GOD'S GRACE FUELS MY PASSION, will encourage you in your walk of faith."

- Pastor Happy Caldwell
President Victory Television Network

"GOD'S GRACE FUELS MY PASSION" is a captivating guide for those of us passionate about living our dreams but certain we can't do it on our own. Anyone desiring a clear-cut manual to walk out your God-given destiny will treasure this resource as Dr. Maureen removes the "pressure to perform" and reveals how to "receive the grace" for your unique race.

- **Terri Savelle Foy**
Terri Savelle Foy Ministries, Rockwall, TX

God's Grace
Fuels My Passion

by

Dr. Maureen Anderson

Second Edition 2019 Published by **The Word for Winners**
P. O. Box 22229
Mesa, AZ 85277
(480) 669-0102

ISBN-10: 1682734536
ISBN-13: 9781682734537

MAUREEN ANDERSON TV
THE WORD FOR WINNERS

God's Grace Fuels My Passion
Dr. Maureen Anderson

Graphic Design Artist: Mendi Glenn
Editor: Shelley Anne Johnson[6]
Proof Copy/Typists: Susan Gross, Brenda Beasley, Kathy Canuel
Gayle Schuch

God's Grace Fuels My Passion
Table of Contents

Acknowledgement

What a wonderful book! Is so powerful. Thank you for allowing me to write the forward. I pray everyone will know how important this message is!

Dr Maureen Anderson is not just a student of the Word of God but like Mary, a lover of the Words of the Lord. That's never more evident than when you read this book, *God's Grace Fuels My Passion*. In her writing, the truth of grace over law, mercy over justice and trust over works become clear as she tells of her own journey from bondage to freedom.

Dr. Maureen exposes the lies of the enemy that keep Jesus-loving people from walking in the truth of the completed work of Christ. Choosing to "let go of the control, let the Holy Spirit be the revealer of your destiny, relax and trust the Holy Spirit" is the first step to real freedom, real peace and real impact in this Christian life.

No matter how long you've known the Grace of God, it is a temptation to begin to rely on your own efforts to reach your destiny. To be, as Dr Maureen puts it, an earner instead of a receiver.

So we all need to hear it again and again. After all, grace is by faith and faith comes by hearing. This wonderful book is absolutely filled with scripture, expounded upon and explained so well.

My friends, I've found that the more grace I walk in, the more I discover there is ALWAYS more! I found myself quoting Dr Maureen's book to friends and family, noting scripture as they came alive through her own personal experiences. This word of grace has increased my faith and impassioned my heart to receive ALL my precious Lord has designed for me.

Enjoy your journey into the Grace of God, the sweetest life there is...

- Kellie Copeland
Kenneth Copeland Ministries, Newark, TX

Foreword

Are you tired of living in the fog of condemnation and shame? Do you want to know what it feels like to be loved just the way you are? In spite of all your mistakes, all your shortcomings, God loves you just as you are.

This book reveals how to walk out of the fog into the light. Get out from under the curse of shame and guilt and into the light of love and acceptance.

This is one of the best books I have ever read on grace. What I love is that it's a "how-to" book. It shows you how to live a life of grace, not just talk about grace.

If you want to feel loved and accepted, read this incredible book!

- **Pastor Scot Anderson**
Living Word Bible Church, Mesa, AZ

Foreword

There is much confusion around the message of grace, and even hesitation sometimes among Christians. Yet it is the message of the New Covenant. It is undeniably the tenant of the Apostle Paul's passion. Grace is the starting line of our Christianity. In graces' simplicity of salvation is the idea that I've earned nothing. In fact, if anything I've earned some good ole fashioned punishment. Yet here forgiveness and eternal life is a gift for anyone who believes? And this gift is just that, a gift, and by its very definition, cannot be worked for lest it be called a wage.

In this book, Dr. Maureen reveals, without exception, that the faith that begs you receive eternity as a gift, will also open all of God's promises: His Promised Land, a new baptism, joint heirs with Christ, authority, and so much more. The blessings of God are by faith? It's a gift! Your Christian life is about to explode into the blessings of God as you learn what grace affords you and why it is yours.

I'm honored to be asked to write a forward for Dr. Maureen Anderson. She is a Bible protégé, a general in the Christian faith, an anointed preaching machine chosen by God to be a mouth piece of His incorruptible Word. I've never met anyone who knows the Bible as my Mom does. She's been memorizing scripture and quoting it since I was five years old. So when the Holy Spirit revealed grace to her, those dormant seeds of the Word of God sprung to life like a rain forest of insight.

In this book, see grace like you have never seen before. If you have been on the fence, wondering about the message of grace, ready yourself for a tidal wave of scripture to push you into the freedoms that are in Christ. Here the plan of God for forgiveness and redemption is revealed. Each power-packed page will have you not only riveted to press on, but invited to read again and again as you squeeze even more out of every word.

\- **Pastor Jason Anderson**
Living Word Bible Church, Mesa, AZ

A Picture of Grace
Chapter 1

My husband, my hero, after spending four committed years in the Navy, received an honorable discharge from the Navy. As he walked down the gang plank from the *USS Mississinewa*, he saluted the flag and the quarter deck, then proceeded to the bus stop just off base, took all his Navy clothes off and put on civilian clothes. He was leaving all resemblance of the Navy way, its regulations, clothing, language, and restrictions behind, and he was entering the freedom of civilian life available through the honorable discharge.

⁶But now we are discharged from the law and have terminated all intercourse with it, having died to what once restrained and held us captive. So now we serve not under [obedience to] the old code of written regulations, but [under obedience to the promptings] of the Spirit in newness [of life]. (Romans 7:6 AMPC)

The Old Covenant was about <u>what we do</u>, and the New Covenant is about what <u>Christ has done</u>.

We have been discharged from the Covenant of Law and set free into the Covenant of Grace by the blood of Jesus. So understand this. When we receive Christ Jesus as our Savior, we become a child of God under the Covenant of Grace. We have been discharged from the Old Covenant of the Law.

1

The Old Covenant was about what we do, and the New Covenant is about what Christ has done.

Paul, by inspiration of the Holy Spirit, tells us that we died to the law or what we do. The law is no more, the law is obsolete. It is gone, dead. We are now married to Christ. We are to let His life flow through us by the Holy Spirit. In doing so, we bear fruit for God. Now what is invisible in the Kingdom becomes visible in our lives.

³Every spiritual blessing in the heavenly realm has already been lavished upon us as a love gift from our wonderful heavenly Father, the Father of our Lord Jesus—all because He sees us wrapped into Christ. This is why we celebrate Him with all our hearts! (Ephesians 1:3 TPT)

These are the love gifts from your wonderful heavenly Father because we now are in grace, being wrapped up in Christ, in Christ's works.

Paul goes on to tell us we are set free from the law, what we do. We step into Christ's greatness because Christ's life is flowing through us to create an amazing life, a life of too much!

Being married to Christ tells us in the fifth chapter of Ephesians that Christ now washes us with the water of the Word.

²⁶...to make us holy and pure, cleansing us through the showering of the pure water of the Word of God. ²⁷All that He does in us is designed to make us a mature church for His pleasure, until we become a source of praise to Him—glorious and radiant, beautiful and holy, without fault or flaw. (Ephesians 5:26-27 TPT)

It's now Christ ministering to me under grace and not my job under law. Grace makes me Christ-conscious and not sin-conscious.

2

Grace is not a license to sin, but the power and ability to not sin, being free from sin's power.

[11]For the grace of God has appeared that offers salvation to all people. [12]It teaches us to say "No" to ungodliness and worldly passions, and to live self-controlled, upright and godly lives in this present age. (Titus 2:11-12 NIV)

Law is the strength of sin or power of sin.

[56]The sting of death is sin, and the power of sin is the law. (1 Corinthians 15:56 NIV)

I don't have power in myself to get out of rejection, out of addictions, out of worthlessness, or out of poverty. Under the law, I try to get out, but only get deeper in. It's like this, I state, "I'm done with desserts!" Only by the fourth day after I make that statement, I am driven to eat the whole cake and everything in sight!

Testimony

When I was a smoker, I would, under my own strength, (I wasn't born again yet) throw all the cigarettes away. By 2:00 am in the morning, I was frantically searching for a cigarette and would even go into the car looking. I couldn't do it myself. When I got born-again, the first thing God said to me was, "You will never smoke again." And by grace, I was instantly set free.

Grace is a mentor, a voice in us that teaches and mentors us to be free from sin, to live a life of freedom from addictions, poverty, sickness, rejection and on and on…a life that's free from the curse.

Grace is a free gift to set me free from the curse, from addictions, and from bad behavior. It's not what I do; it's what Christ has done. Grace makes me a receiver to what I already have in Christ. Isn't this exciting, good news?

You are free, and now stand in your freedom. Don't again get under bondage of the law that put you under the curse. Those under Jewish Law were telling the Galatians they must get under Jewish Law to be saved. The Apostle Paul, by the Holy Spirit, was telling them, "You can't mix the law with grace. You will put yourself back under the curse." He further states:

[7]Yet you have allowed those who mingle law with grace to confuse you with lies. (Galatians 1:7b TPT)

Christ did a complete work, and you can't add anything to it.
If you do, then it's not grace.

Paul is saying, "It won't work!" Why? Because Christ did a complete work, and you can't add anything to it. If you do, then it's not grace. Paul says to the church in Galatians, "If they preach this to you, let them be condemned." Paul, by the Holy Spirit, is very serious about the life of grace and what it really means.

[8]For it is by grace you have been saved, through faith – and this is not from yourselves, it is the gift of God – [9]not by works, so that no one can boast. (Ephesians 2:8-9 NIV)

By grace, by the works of Christ, you are saved and you can't add to it. It's God's free gift to us, so we can't boast. It's all Christ! None of me, but I have to believe and receive the death, burial and resurrection of Christ, the Gospel of Grace. As Jesus said on the cross, "It is finished." Once I receive the

4

free gifts, I become a child of God into His life *and life more abundantly.* (John 10:10 NKJ)

As we enter into the Kingdom of God, just as the church in Galatia, we can have a legalistic mindset that says we have "to do" to get God's love. We have "to do" to get God's favor. We have "to do" to earn God's acceptance. We must understand that the devil is a legalist and keeps putting more and more law on us. We allow it because the image of God on the inside of us is legalistic toward God.

I experienced this myself right after I got saved. We attended a legalistic church, and I fell right into the law and more. I went through the Bible to find all the don'ts and thought, "I've got this! I will be the best! God will be so pleased with me." Now, in this church everything was sin except eating. At the age of 25, I looked embarrassing to the world with my culottes to my ankles. (Shorts and pants were a sin in that church.) I was no witness under the law. And of course, under the law, if you break one law, you broke them all. Now in my own deceived mind, I thought I was doing great, but I wasn't. (Only Jesus does great.) So we went from poverty, to me being sick most of the time, to rejection, to depression and on and on it went.

[10]For all who rely on the works of the law are under a curse, as it is written: "Cursed is everyone who does not continue to do everything written in the Book of the Law." [11]Clearly no one who relies on the law is justified before God, because "the righteous will live by faith." (Galatians 3:10-11 NIV)

In the Book of Job, we see two covenants, the Old Covenant of the Law and the New Covenant of Grace. Job starts out as a picture of someone who is totally committed to the law. Job, under the law, was "doing" to be righteous, "doing" to be holy and totally depending on himself to earn right standing with God. Under the law, we become more and more fanatical about the law, and we see this in Job. Job got so extreme that he began offering sacrifices for his children in case they had sinned.

⁵When a period of feasting had run its course, Job would make arrangements for them to be purified. Early in the morning he would sacrifice a burnt offering for each of them, thinking, "Perhaps my children have sinned and cursed God in their hearts." This was Job's regular custom. (Job 1:5 NIV)

Job was was totally committed to the law. Under the law, you are afraid of doing something wrong. So, you become fear driven, and you know the law speaks of punishment. Fear demands more fear.

¹⁸There is no fear in love. But perfect love drives out fear... (1 John 4:18 NIV)

See, the law can become addictive, and you can find yourself repenting for things you never did just in case you thought it. That's what the law does. It's fear driven.

²⁵For the thing I greatly feared has come upon me, and what I dreaded has happened to me. (Job 3:25 NKJ)

So what Job feared the most, came upon him.

When you're sin conscious, you depend on you.
When you're Christ conscious, you depend on Christ.

You can't satisfy the law. You become what you look at, and if it's sin, you become more sin conscious. If it's Christ, you become more and more Christ conscious. When you're sin conscious, you depend on you. When you're Christ conscious, you depend on Christ.

Look at Job's life. We are imperfect, and the law is good and holy, but we can't keep it. The law was given to show us we needed a Redeemer, a Savior. So under the law, the devil had an open door to bring the curse on Job. Satan is a legalist, and keeps us in a life of fear. God said, "Look at Job." No matter how hard Job tried, he couldn't do everything right and perfect. God had bound Himself to His Word. So if you break one law, you broke them all. Job thought he could keep the law in and of himself. He didn't see that he needed a Savior.

How many of us are like Job? We think we can keep the law. We get saved and then put ourselves under the law.

12 But keeping the law does not require faith, but self-effort. For the law teaches, "If you practice the principles of law, you must follow all of them." (Galatians 3:12 TPT)

Keeping the law doesn't require faith because Jesus is the starter of my faith, the beginner of my faith. Jesus was the only One Who could keep all the law, the only perfect One. Jesus came to fulfill the law.

Job's friends tried to put more law on Job. God was not happy about that.

7After the Lord had said these things to Job, he said to Eliphaz the Temanite, "I am angry with you and your two friends, because you have not spoken the truth about Me, as my servant Job has." (Job 42:7 NIV)

Now Job finally comes to his senses and realizes that he needs a Savior and cries out, *"My Redeemer lives!"* We see Job step out of the law that brought the curse and step into the New Covenant of Grace that depends on a Savior and brings the blessings.

25For I know that my Redeemer lives. (Job 19:25 NKJ)

Job cries out for a redeemer. We also get to the point where we are done with the law, and we cry out for a redeemer.

Things begin to change then. Under the New Covenant of Grace, we get twice as many blessings.

¹⁰And the Lord restored Job's losses when he prayed for his friends. Indeed the Lord gave Job twice as much as he had before.

¹²Now the Lord blessed the latter days of Job more than his beginning; for he had fourteen thousand sheep, six thousand camels, one thousand yoke of oxen, and one thousand female donkeys. ¹³He also had seven sons and three daughters. ¹⁴And he called the name of the first Jemimah, the name of the second Keziah, and the name of the third Keren-Happuch. ¹⁵In all the land were found no women so beautiful as the daughters of Job; and their father gave them an inheritance among their brothers. ¹⁶After this Job lived one hundred and forty years, and saw his children and grandchildren for four generations. (Job 42:10, 12-16 NKJ)

In the new Covenant of Grace, the daughters also inherit the blessings.

¹⁵Nowhere in all the land were there found women as beautiful as Job's daughters, and their father granted them an inheritance along with their brothers. (Job 42:15 NIV)

---

*The Old Covenant is blessings and curses,
but the New Covenant is blessings and blessings.*

There is a picture here, that the latter, the New Covenant of Grace, is better than the Old Covenant of the law.

¹²The Lord blessed the latter part of Job's life more than the former part. He had fourteen thousand sheep, six thousand camels, a thousand yoke of oxen and a thousand donkeys. (Job 42:12 NIV)

The Old Covenant is blessings and curses, but the New Covenant is blessings and blessings. Because the New Covenant depends totally on the works of Christ, and since we are in Christ, we go from blessing to blessing.

[16]*From the fullness of His grace we have all received one blessing after another.* (John 1:16 NIV84)

In the New Covenant the blessings are working for you.

Legalism is a very sneaky thing and is the direct opposite of grace. It creeps in, and soon believers think they are "more spiritual" because of what they do or don't do. In law, there is bondage because there is no power to get free from bad behavior, addictions, or generational curses. In the Spirit, there is liberty. This is the power for freedom from bad behavior, addictions, and generational curses. It's the power to go from blessing to blessing, from life to more abundant life, from royalty to royalty, etc. Christ provided all the blessing for us in the life of grace.

Now grace doesn't make you lazy.

[10]*But by the grace of God I am what I am, and His grace to me was not without effect. No, I worked harder than all of them—yet not I, but the grace of God that was with me.* (1 Corinthians 15:10 NIV)

Grace is an empowerment. It's a supernatural energy that empowers you. It's a force that carries you in your race to fulfill God's destiny for you. Grace propels you ahead.

[8]*This superabundant grace is already powerfully working in us.* (Ephesians 1:8 TPT)

[20]*Never doubt God's mighty power to work in you and accomplish all this. He will achieve infinitely more than your greatest request, your most unbelievable dream, and exceed your wildest imagination! He will outdo them all, for His*

miraculous power constantly energizes you. (Ephesians 3:20 TPT)

You aren't lazy! But instead you are so full of the power and energy of God. His life has so consumed you, that you can't stop building, doing, and going with passion, love and joy.

⁹*My passion is to enlighten every person to this divine mystery.* (Ephesians 3:9 TPT)

God's grace fuels my passion because Christ's supernatural power is working in us.

Now our Apostle Paul is identifying himself. Paul knew who he was in Christ.

¹*My name is Paul and I have been commissioned as an apostle of the Lord Jesus, the Messiah. My apostleship was not granted to me by any council of men, for I was appointed by Jesus, the Anointed One, and God the Father, Who raised Him from the dead.* (Galatians 1:1 TPT)

We need to know who we are in Christ, our identity in Him. Before the creation of the world, He created you to be holy in Him.

⁴*For He chose us in Him before the creation of the world to be holy and blameless in His sight.* (Ephesians 1:4 NIV)

The Word of God says He is the Alpha and the Omega.

⁸*"I am the Alpha and the Omega," says the Lord God, "Who is, and Who was, and Who is to come, the Almighty."* (Revelation 1:8 NIV)

There is no time in the invisible to God. God started, then He finished, then He began. God has already run your race and finished it. And now God gives it to you to have a free will to choose His destiny for you. Or you can choose your own destiny, but in His destiny for you, you are a winner. God already gave you everything to be amazing.

[16]Your eyes saw my unformed body; all the days ordained for me were written in Your book before one of them came to be. (Psalm 139:16 NIV)

So in Him, you relax. God set you up to be successful in Him.

[11]Through our union with Christ we too have been claimed by God as His own inheritance. Before we were even born, He gave us our destiny; that we would fulfill the plan of God Who always accomplishes every purpose and plan in His heart. (Ephesians 1:11 TPT)

Now our part is to receive the book He wrote about us, give up our book and fulfill His destiny for us. We need to come to know who we are in Christ by His Word, and the Holy Spirit is here to reveal it to us. So we don't have to be stressed out about destiny. Who am I? What is my destiny? That is legalistic thinking.

We don't have to be stressed out about our destiny.

Let go, and receive the destiny you already have in the invisible. Let it become visible through embracing it and allowing it to flow through you. Let go, and let the Holy Spirit do His job.

[6]...being confident of this, that He Who began a good work in you will carry it on to completion until the day of Christ Jesus. (Philippians 1:6 NIV)

He began the good work, and He will complete it. Enter into the truth of this scripture, and trust Him that He doesn't lie. Allow Him to be the boss. Relax and receive.

We get so stressed out in our own human effort of doing, doing, doing, and saying, "I don't want to miss God!" "Will I miss God?" Worry, worry. Get into grace and receive destiny. Trust it's already done in Him.

Testimony

I was one of those worriers about destiny. I went ahead and planned my destiny by what I saw in the natural and in the midst of it all, God revealed His plan to me. Guess what? It wasn't what I had planned. Even when we think we have to plan it and make it happen, God is faithful to reveal His plan in grace.

This is what my plan looked like. Since I was traveling at that time, speaking for Women's Aglow and churches, I began to plan my life around that. And while I was planning my destiny, God visited me in a dream and told me I was called to build a church with my husband. Then it happened by the power of God and not by my own doing! As the church started, (Believe me, it was supernatural!) I was still traveling and speaking for Women's Aglow and other churches. One day in prayer God spoke to my heart and said, "You can travel and speak or you can build the church, but you can't do both. I've called you to build the church."

God's plan was totally different from my plan. What I am trying to say here is, relax and receive God's destiny for you in the season you are in. Trust God is faithful to reveal it to you by the Holy Spirit.

I have finished the church season, and God has been <u>more</u> than faithful to bring me into the next season in my life. He is faithful. Enter into His rest and let the Holy Spirit do what He has been sent to do. We don't need to figure out our destiny. We just need to trust the Holy Spirit to do it. And even if we mess up, the Holy Spirit is faithful to fix it. Let Him!

You were not made by a cookie cutter.
You are a custom-made, unique, one-of-a-kind
destiny-planned-from-the-beginning-of-time child of God!

You were not made by a cookie cutter. You are a custom-made, unique, one-of-a-kind, destiny-planned-from-the-beginning-of-time child of God! You are special, and God's destiny for you for the season you are in is always bigger then you. You need God.

¹³for it is God Who works in you to will and to act in order to fulfill His good purpose. (Philippians 2:13 NIV)

This scripture points out that God has already fulfilled it in the unseen, (in you) and it can't fail in Him. This is what grace means, that Christ did it all. You are to just walk in His works.

²⁴The One Who calls you is faithful, and He will do it. (1 Thessalonians 5:24 NIV)

God called you, and He is faithful to work His purpose through you. Let me tell you what your part is. It's surrender, believe and receive, and let it flow through you. Now this is the plan that Jesus shows us in the Gospel, the "how to's" of grace living.

³⁰By myself I can do nothing. (John 5:30 NIV)

Jesus was saying that He can't heal or do miracles in or of Himself. It's Father God, in Him, flowing through Him and doing them.

²⁸*So Jesus said, "When you have lifted up the Son of Man, then you will know that I am He and that I do nothing on My own but speak just what the Father has taught Me.* (John 8:28 NIV)

Jesus never taught. It was Father God speaking through Jesus.

¹⁶*Jesus answered, "My teaching is not My own. It comes from the One Who sent Me.* (John 7:16 NIV)

This is very important to the grace life. Jesus is giving us a picture of when He walked this earth that it wasn't Him, but Father God flowing through Him Who was laying hands on the sick. It was Father God teaching through Him. It was Father God doing all the miracles through Him. Jesus was totally submitted to God, letting God work through Him.

⁴*Remain in Me, as I also remain in you. No branch can bear fruit by itself; it must remain in the vine. Neither can you bear fruit unless you remain in Me.* ⁵*I am the vine; you are the branches. If you remain in Me and I in you, you will bear much fruit; apart from Me you can do nothing.* (John 15:4-5 NIV)

Jesus is saying to us here, "This is how I walked this earth. Now you imitate me. It's not you, but it's Me in you that will heal the sick, raise the dead, open the blind eyes. It's Me in you that will do miracles and set the captives free. It's not you, it's Me Who will teach through you. Let grace flow through you."

We can get so stressed out with our legalistic thinking. I have to do, do, do, instead of grace thinking, Jesus did, did, did!

When Jesus walked this earth, He rested in the works of God to flow through Him. Now we are the branch, and the only life in the branch is the life of the vine that flows through the branch to produce fruit. This is a picture of the grace life.

Holy Spirit, Revealer of Our Destiny
Chapter 2

The grace of God (what Christ has done) binds us to the blessings of God that are working for us. The law (what we do) binds us to the curse. We are now born-again believers.

As we travel and minister the Covenant of Grace, we find people who have spent their whole lives under the teachings of legalism and religion. They have so much fear in letting go and trusting in grace. It's as though they think they can keep themselves from sin. What a lie! They are trusting in themselves not to sin instead of trusting in God's grace, what Christ has done, to keep them from sinning. We must wake up to the truth that the power of sin is the law.

56...the power of sin is the law. (1 Corinthians 15:56 NIV)

Grace has the power and ability to keep us from sinning.

Grace has the power and ability to keep us from sinning. It's what Christ has already done.

11For the grace of God has appeared that offers salvation to all people. 12It teaches us to say "No" to ungodliness and worldly passions, and to live self-controlled, upright and godly lives in this present age. (Titus 2:11-12 NIV)

Under the law, we go from one bad thing to the next. We never see the blessings of God working for us. We are fear driven, not faith driven. The law is holy and perfect, but we are not. Jesus is the only One Who could keep the law. Jesus is the only One Who is perfect. We are now in Christ. Grace abides in us. Grace is the power of God, that voice of God that teaches and mentors us, gives us the power to say "no" to sin. Grace is a force of God that teaches us to have an upright, self-controlled, godly life. We love grace's power and ability that is working in us to set us up for success. Grace brings us into God's love, passion, life, and life more abundant.

Paul had a revelation of grace. In all his writings by the Holy Spirit, he was continually saying, "Come out of the law and into the life of grace." He was continually teaching in the churches that we have been freed from the law to live the life of grace.

[18]The law, then, doesn't supersede the promise since the royal proclamation was given before the law. If that were the case, it would have nullified what God said to Abraham. We receive all the promises because of the Promised One—not because we keep the law! (Galatians 3:18 TPT)

All the promises have been deeded to us, signed over to us. We receive all of the promises because of the Promised One (Jesus). Understand it's because of what Christ has done. He paid our penalty in full. Jesus took all our sin to the cross. Jesus totally set us free. He did a complete work for us by His death, burial, and resurrection. This was so we could have eternal life and live in all the blessings of God, not because we keep the law. We don't receive the blessings by keeping the law. It's not by human effort, but it's in His life, His works. The Word of God says,

[28]For in Him we live and move and have our being. (Acts 17:28 NIV)

[17]...as He is, so are we in this world. (1 John 4:17 NIV)

Jesus was showing us how to live the life of grace because Jesus was full of grace.

¹⁶From the fullness of His grace we have all received one blessing after another. (John 1:16 NIV84)

Jesus states that in grace we just go from blessing to blessing in life.

³⁰By Myself I can do nothing... (John 5:30 NIV)

Jesus was saying here that by Himself He could do nothing. He is showing us in grace when He got baptized in the River Jordan and the Holy Spirit came upon Him, it was now the Holy Spirit (in Him) flowing through Him Who was healing the sick, opening the blind eyes, raising the dead, and doing signs and wonders. God was flowing through Him preaching the Word.

¹⁶Jesus answered, "My teaching is not My own. It comes from the One Who sent Me." (John 7:16 NIV)

²⁸So Jesus said, "When you have lifted up the Son of Man, then you will know that I am He and that I do nothing on My own but speak just what the Father has taught Me." (John 8:28 NIV)

Jesus is showing us that when we get born again, we need to let Him flow through us to heal the sick, to open the blind eyes, to raise the dead, to do signs and wonders and preach the Word of Grace, Christ in us the hope of glory.

²⁷...Christ in you, the hope of glory. (Colossians 1:27 NIV)

⁵I am the vine; you are the branches. If you remain in Me and I in you, you will bear much fruit; apart from Me you can do nothing. (John 15:5 NIV)

What is Jesus saying to us here? In the Kingdom of God, being born again, we must realize we can't, but Jesus has done it. It's finished in the Kingdom. Jesus is saying, "It's Me Who is going to flow through you by the Holy Spirit, It's Me Who is going to bear much fruit through you as you surrender to Me, and let Me flow through you." Jesus shows us the way of life in the Covenant of Grace. This is entering into the rest of God, believing it's done, receiving it and then letting it flow through us!

Let's look at the day of Pentecost. Peter spoke this:

²²Fellow Israelites, listen to this: Jesus of Nazareth was a man accredited by God to you by miracles, wonders and signs, which God did among you through Him, as you yourselves know. (Acts 2:22 NIV)

God finished your destiny in the invisible.

Peter had the revelation of God flowing through Jesus to do miracles, signs and wonders. It was God through Jesus Who did the supernatural. Peter understood the Covenant of Grace, the New Covenant.

When we understand the Covenant of Grace by revelation, we can then enter into the rest of God. God is the Alpha and Omega, the Beginning and the End. God began and then finished and then began. God finished your destiny in the invisible. Then He put it in you to believe what He did, to receive it and let it flow through you.

¹¹Through our union with Christ we too have been claimed by God as His own inheritance. Before we were even born, He gave us our destiny; that we would fulfill the plan of God Who always accomplishes every purpose and plan in His heart. (Ephesians 1:11 TPT)

Take what is invisible in God's heart and make it visible in your life, the amazing life He planned for you!

29Take My yoke upon you and learn from Me, for I am gentle and humble in heart, and you will find rest for your souls. 30For My yoke is easy and My burden is light. (Matthew 11:29-30 NIV)

Take <u>His</u> yoke upon you.

Testimony

Since I was 27 years old, I've often run children's ministries. I've loved it, and I've loved the children, but the problem was being able to get enough help. It was always difficult having to beg people to help. It was an overload. It just made me not want to run it, and I prayed and fasted and nothing changed much. It stole the joy out of my heart.

When I came into the revelation of the Covenant of Grace, the Holy Spirit through the Scriptures revealed to me that before He created, He already finished destiny for the children's ministry. Now through prayer I needed to receive God's helpers, His divine connection for His purpose with the children. After that prayer of faith, and for the first time, I had too much! I had too many helpers to build the children's ministry. These are over-the-top amazing people.

In grace, God always goes beyond what you are asking. In grace, all I have to do is receive what I already have in the unseen. Under my legalistic mindset, I was trying to get <do, do, do.> So, now my prayer in grace is this:

> *Father God, before the foundation of time You already picked the team, You put destiny in those You have chosen to work in Children's Church, and I believe it. I receive them from*

wherever they live on this earth, only those You have chosen for divine connection for your purpose, in Jesus Name.

And God did it! Yay!

²Ask the Lord of the harvest, therefore, to send out workers into His harvest field. (Luke 10:2 NIV)

He already has them waiting for us to believe and receive. When we pray like this, the Holy Spirit begins to move on them through dreams, visions, thoughts, desires, and passion. The gifts of the Holy Spirit are released to flow to bring them into the Children's Ministry.

This is the scripture to meditate on until it becomes a reality in your heart.

³Every spiritual blessing in the heavenly realm has already been lavished upon us as a love gift from our wonderful heavenly Father, the Father of our Lord Jesus—all because He sees us wrapped into Christ. This is why we celebrate Him with all our hearts! (Ephesians 1:3 TPT)

Stop and let this soak in.
Everything heaven contains has already been lavished on you!

Stop and let this soak in. Everything heaven contains has already been lavished on you. <u>Already</u> means you already have it in the unseen. Now your part is to embrace it as done. Why? Because the Father God see's you wrapped in Christ.

Get the vision that before you were born, God already put destiny in you. God wrote a book about you.

Paul, the Apostle, stated that before he was even born, God had called him to be an apostle and to preach to the Gentiles the Covenant of Grace.

¹My name is Paul and I have been commissioned as an apostle of the Lord Jesus, the Messiah. My apostleship was not granted to me by any council of men, for I was appointed by Jesus, the Anointed One, and God the Father, Who raised Him from the dead. (Galatians 1:1 TPT)

¹²No one taught me this revelation, for it was given to me directly by the unveiling of Jesus the Anointed One. (Galatians 1:12 TPT)

¹⁵But then God called me by His grace; and in love, He chose me from my birth to be His. ¹⁶God's grace unveiled His Son in me so that I would proclaim Him to the non-Jewish people of the world. After I had this encounter I kept it a secret for some time, sharing it with no one. (Galatians 1:15-16 TPT)

God put destiny in us, and set us up to be successful. He already did it! He already made us successful in Christ. We always have the freedom to choose God's way or our way.

The Holy Spirit is the revealer of your destiny. It's the Holy Spirit's part to reveal it to you. Your part is to surrender to the plan, receive it, and let Christ flow through you.

²⁷...the Holy Spirit passionately pleads before God for us, His holy ones, in perfect harmony with God's plan and our destiny. (Romans 8:27 TPT)

The Holy Spirit in you is your GPS (Global Positioning System) for God's will. Jesus told us He would not leave us as orphans. He would send the Holy Spirit to us.

¹⁷ ...the Spirit of truth. The world cannot accept Him, because it neither sees Him nor knows Him. But you know Him, for He lives with you and will be in you. ¹⁸I will not leave you as orphans; I will come to you. (John 14:17-18 NIV)

The Holy Spirit is going to be your Guide, your Comforter. He will show you the way. That's His job in your life. Let go and let God! One of our biggest problems as believers is that we don't trust the Holy Spirit to do His job. We think we have to do it. <Do, do, do again.> It's either the Holy Spirit or you. It can't be both. We can't mix law (what you do) and grace (what Christ has already done). It won't work.

Get that paradigm shift in your mind. God is setting you free to trust Him with your destiny.

⁹However, as it is written:

What no eye has seen, what no ear has heard, and what no human mind has conceived—the things God has prepared for those who love Him— ¹⁰these are the things God has revealed to us by His Spirit. The Spirit searches all things, even the deep things of God. ¹²What we have received is not the spirit of the world, but the Spirit Who is from God, so that we may understand what God has freely given us. (1 Corinthians 2:9-10, 12 NIV)

Paul is saying to them, "Give it up!" What do we think about the Holy Spirit? That He can't do His job? That He is going to forget about us? Come on! The Holy Spirit is faithful to the call of God, and has the power and ability to do a great job in your life! And if you go the wrong way, the Holy Spirit will tell you.

²¹Whether you turn to the right or to the left, your ears will hear a voice behind you, saying, "This is the way; walk in it." (Isaiah 30:21 NIV)

When you let go of the control, let the Holy Spirit be the revealer of your destiny, relax and trust the Holy Spirit, then things will be revealed to your spirit.

The Holy Spirit is not weird, but naturally spiritual in you. In our natural sense, we will not find what our purpose is, or how we are to run our business or where there is danger in the natural realm. It's not going to happen. What the Word of

God is saying is in the natural realm, we won't find destiny. How do we find our destiny? It's only by the Holy Spirit. The Holy Spirit will reveal it to you. The Holy Spirit is in your life to reveal God's plan for you.

The Holy Spirit is in your life to reveal God's plan for you.

Can I trust the Holy Spirit to lead me? Can I really? Our intellect takes over, and we think, "That looks great!" And then we go the way of the intellect only to find out it's the wrong way. We shouldn't have gone that way. The Scripture goes on to say that the Holy Spirit searches all things. Why? This is the Holy Spirit's purpose in your life, to reveal even the deep things of God, for you personally. We have not received the spirit of the world. With the spirit of the world, you do, you do, you do. The Spirit of God is He did, He did, He did. Why? So you will understand what God has freely given you. So you will understand your destiny. What you are to step into in the Kingdom to receive from Him, and let it flow through you to build His kingdom with victory, success, and ease. For now grace is carrying it and you. For whatever He shows you, it's already done in the unseen. Now you connect to it, and it becomes visible in your world. This is how, in grace, I live my life, and God does one miracle after another.

[10]*But by the grace of God I am what I am, and His grace to me was not without effect. No, I worked harder than all of them—yet not I, but the grace of God that was with me.* (1 Corinthians 15:10 NIV)

It's not your job to find your destiny. Let it go, and let the Holy Spirit be the revealer of your destiny. That's your paradigm shift!

⁹And through the revelation of the Anointed One, He unveiled His secret desires to us – the hidden mystery of His long-range plan, which He was delighted to implement from the very beginning of time. (Ephesians 1:9 TPT)

Let's look at these Scriptures. They are secrets, but the Holy Spirit unveils those secrets to us. What secrets? The hidden plans that God has for your life. They are hidden, but in the Holy Spirit they are revealed to you. They are not hidden any more.

God delights to implement our destiny. Now, a legalistic mindset says, "It's our responsibility to find God's plan for our lives," but Christ already did it! It's the Holy Spirit's responsibility to reveal God's plan for us. We can be so focused and stressed in doing and finding the right plan, that we miss it because of law, what I must do. The new Grace Covenant is receiving what is already done. We need to let go of the control, and let the Holy Spirit take control. It's a trust issue.

I meet people all the time who can't let go of the control, and they are in a tizzy. "What do I do? What do I do? What do I do? What's my purpose?" Relax and let God, and trust the Holy Spirit! He will put you in your lane.

When we surrender to grace, we effortlessly fulfill the plan He has for us with great joy because grace is working through us to do it. Never doubt the energy in grace. Grace is His energy, His power, His passion working in us. When we surrender to grace we get a high in God. Since I came into the revelation of grace, I have so much energy and passion. I'm so excited about every day! I'm living the dream - life and life more abundant, going from blessing to blessing.

God's Timing is Now
Chapter 3

Grace makes you a receiver and law makes you an earner.

29Take my yoke upon you and learn from me, for I am gentle and humble in heart, and you will find rest for your souls. 30For my yoke is easy and my burden is light." (Matthew 11:29-30 NIV)

What is His yoke? It's His grace. *"And learn from Me."* It's the voice of the Holy Spirit because the Word of God tells us:

11For the grace of God has appeared that offers salvation to all people. 12It teaches us to say "No" to ungodliness and worldly passions, and to live self-controlled, upright and godly lives in this present age... (Titus 2:11-12 NIV)

Grace is the voice of the Holy Spirit that tells us to say no to ungodliness and worldly passions. Grace gives us ability and power to be free of addictions, being totally delivered. Grace is the voice of the Holy Spirit to teach, and to mentor. It's the voice that brings revelation, opens the Word of God to us and its hidden secrets.

What does it mean that Jesus was *"humble in heart?"* Jesus always gave all the credit to Father God. Jesus was saying, "I am totally submitted to Father God for God's power to flow through Me and out of Me to touch this world as I walk the earth." We learn how to let Jesus' power flow through us and out of us to touch the lives around us. Our testimony should be, *"In Him I live and move and have my being.* (Acts 17:38) I'm totally surrendered to Him."

At the core of grace is a life that Jesus already did. It's me surrendering to the destiny He already put in me that He finished in the unseen. It's a life of believing, receiving and letting it flow through me. This is where we find rest for our souls. God's Kingdom is a Kingdom of Faith. In faith there is no time. We step into the unseen, and in the unseen, it's finished. This is where God lives. This is why it's not about what I do, but what Jesus has done.

At the core of grace is a life that Jesus already did.

---

³Every spiritual blessing in the heavenly realm has already been lavished upon us as a love gift from our wonderful heavenly Father, the Father of our Lord Jesus—all because He sees us wrapped into Christ. This is why we celebrate Him with all our hearts! (Ephesians 1:3 TPT)

In the invisible, I must see that everything in heaven has already been lavished upon me. It's a love gift from Father God. It's nothing I earned. I already have it. I have the Kingdom of God in me, the Godhead in bodily form in me. I am a spirit made in His likeness and image. I have a soul that contains my mind, will, emotions and subconscious, and I live in a body. Now, the old man died when I became born again, but guess what? The old man left junk behind like doubt and unbelief, like addictions, rejection and so much more. But that's not who I am!

¹⁹For I do not do the good I want to do, but the evil I do not want to do—this I keep on doing. ²⁰Now if I do what I do not want to do, it is no longer I who do it, but it is sin living in me that does it. (Romans 7:19-20 NIV)

So, I must be able to identify who I am in Christ, made in His image and likeness. But in the soul (mind, will, emotions, subconscious) there is stuff that was left behind, and that stuff is not me, so I don't identify with it. I'm not sin conscious (looking for sin in me), but I let the Holy Spirit do the cleanup with the understanding that it's His call to reveal stuff to me. It's not my call.

9But if we freely admit our sins when His light uncovers them, He will be faithful to forgive us every time. (1 John 1:9 TPT)

9However, as it is written: "What no eye has seen, what no ear has heard, and what no human mind has conceived" - the things God has prepared for those who love Him - 10these are the things God has revealed to us by His Spirit.

The Spirit searches all things, even the deep things of God. 11For who knows a person's thoughts except their own spirit within them? In the same way no one knows the thoughts of God except the Spirit of God. 12What we have received is not the spirit of the world, but the Spirit Who is from God, so that we may understand what God has freely given us. (1Corinthians 2:9-12 NIV)

By these scriptures we must realize that it's not our job to go looking for the junk the "old man" left behind. It's the Holy Spirit's job and power. Our place is letting go and allowing the Holy Spirit do His work.

It's that legalistic mindset that says, "I have to do! I have to do!" By thinking this way, we take away the Holy Spirit's job in our lives. The Holy Spirit is the One Who searches all things and reveals them to us. (1 Corinthians 2:10)

The Holy Spirit is very detailed in your destiny. He searches it all out, and reveals it to you. The Word tells us that the Spirit makes known to us what God has freely given to us.

(1 Corinthians 2:12) Who makes it known? It's not you. It's the Holy Spirit's responsibility to search it out and reveal it to you.

We can have this strange image of the Holy Spirit that makes Him weird. He is not! The Holy Spirit is really normal in your life. It's that still, quiet voice that has many facets to it in which to lead us. And when we go the wrong way, He will always let us know.

This is a trust issue in our lives. God is saying to us,

"Make the paradigm shift! It's not your job, so let go, and let the Holy Spirit do His job in your life. The Holy Spirit isn't sleeping on the job. He didn't forget you. He didn't take a vacation. Do you think He doesn't do a great job?"

Let the Holy Spirit do His job in your life.
He isn't sleeping on the job. He didn't forget you.

Jesus said in John 14 that He must go to the Father so He could send the Holy Spirit, the Spirit of Truth. He said,

[18]*I will not leave you as orphans.* (John 14:18 NKJ)

An orphan doesn't have any guidance or direction because he has no parents. Jesus sent you the Holy Spirit to be your guide, your direction, your comforter, your revealer of truth, your teacher, for you personally. It's time to let the Holy Spirit do His job.

[29]*Take My yoke upon you and learn from Me, for I am gentle and humble in heart, and you will find rest for your souls.* [30]*For My yoke is easy and My burden is light.* (Matthew 11:29-30 NIV)

Take the yoke of grace on. Let grace (the voice of the Holy Spirit) teach you, that you might learn to find rest for your soul. No more worry or anxiety. You win! His burden is light. When we take on <u>our own yoke,</u> what we have to do and earn, we get into performance…what I've got to earn, what I've got to do, do, and do, so God will love me, and I will fulfill my destiny.

Let it go! It's too heavy. You aren't capable of carrying it or the responsibility that goes with it. All you have to do is choose. You always have freedom of choice. God put destiny in you before you were born. It's in there!

God predestined everyone for heaven, but not everyone will choose it. God wants all to come to the saving knowledge of Jesus, to be born again. (1 Timothy 2:4)

Will you connect to the destiny God has put in you or will you choose your way? We have a free will to choose. We can choose life or death, blessings or curses. We choose.

When we surrender to grace, we effortlessly fulfill the plan God has for us with great joy. It's because grace is working through us to do destiny that's already done in the unseen. The Word of God instructs us to never doubt the energy in grace.

[20]Never doubt God's mighty power to work in you and accomplish all this. He will achieve infinitely more that your greatest request, your most unbelievable dream, and exceed your wildest imagination! He will outdo them all, for His miraculous power constantly energizes you. (Ephesians 3:20 TPT)

[11]Before we were even born, He gave us our destiny; that we would fulfill the plan of God Who always accomplishes every purpose and plan in His heart. (Ephesians 1:11 TPT)

We are making a paradigm shift! Before you were born, God accomplished your destiny in His heart <in the unseen>. God saw your destiny done in His heart. Then He put it in you before you were born, but God already accomplished it. All you have to do now is believe it, receive it done, and let the power of agreement bring it into the seen realm by your choice.

I can choose it or not. It's up to me because of free will. Grace doesn't make you lazy as Paul said,

[10] *"I worked harder than all of them - yet not I, but the grace of God that was with me."* (1 Corinthians 15:10 NIV)

Paul was stating, "It's not me, but grace!" Grace is energy that causes you to enter into God's rest. You go from blessing to blessing.

So under grace, it is not our place to find God's will, but rather to rest in the confidence that the Holy Spirit reveals God's will to us.

[6] *...being confident of this, that He Who began a good work in you will carry it on to completion until the day of Christ Jesus.* (Philippians 1:6 NIV)

Say this, "I let the Holy Spirit reveal God's will to me."

Faith opens the way to enter into the life of grace.

Let's talk about faith. Faith opens the way to enter into the life of grace. So, we must understand faith.

[2] *...through Whom we have gained access by faith into this grace in which we now stand...* (Romans 5:2 NIV)

Faith is in the now. When we step into the unseen, there is no time.

[11] *Now faith is the substance of things hoped for, the evidence of things not seen.* (Hebrews 11:1 NKJ)

We enter into faith that is always now. Hope is in the future. In faith we see it done now. We see it finished now.

Testimony

While we were in our last church building, we bought the property that we are in today. But we had to sell the building we were occupying first in order to build this building. We got a realtor and did all the things we needed to do, but nothing was happening year after year for four years! The religious statement we proclaimed over and over again was, "It just isn't God's timing."

The Holy Spirit began to speak to us that in faith it is now. It's already done. So God began to show us that when we put the building in the future, we weren't in faith. We had to bring it into the now. When we brought it into the now, within just a few weeks, the building was sold!

When we say "It's not God's timing," that is not faith. We need to make a paradigm shift, and get free of that stinking thinking.

35Do you not say, "There are still four months and then comes the harvest?" Behold, I say to you, lift up your eyes and look at the fields, for they are already white for harvest! (John 4:35 NKJ)

Our words have power in them so Jesus was saying, "Don't say it's in the future. Get into faith and see it done. See the harvest done now!"

We see this in the Book of Ezra. During Ezra's time, the Jewish exiles headed to Jerusalem to rebuild the temple. God called them to rebuild it. It was time. They worked hard in laying the foundation. They were so excited that they had an over-the-top celebration, and right after the celebration, the enemy came against them with full force. They were so overwhelmed that they said, "It's just not the timing of God to go on." They left the new foundation they had just laid untouched for 14 years. After 14 years, God had had enough! They had been sent to Jerusalem by God to build the temple.

When the storm came at Ezra and his men, they quit for 14 years. Of course, we have never done that. Quit and said, "It's just not God's timing." But they did! Legalistic thinking is, "It's in the future." Faith thinking is, "It's now! I already have it!"

God came to Ezekiel.

25 *"For I am the LORD: I speak, and the word that I shall speak shall come to pass; it shall no more be prolonged: for in your days, O rebellious house, will I say the word, and will perform it," saith the Lord GOD.* (Ezekiel 12:25 KJV)

Now what are we saying today? "It's not God's timing." There's no difference in what they were saying in Ezekiel's time, and what we are saying today. God is saying to Ezekiel, "This is not Who I Am."

The word *prolonged* in that Scripture is *arak* and means: setback, delayed or postponed. They were saying that every vision, chosen destiny, word of God, fails (*abad* - destroyed, given up as lost, vanished) and now it's been 14 years. God is saying,

"This isn't true! I speak a word, and I do it! When I say, 'It's already done in My heart, in the unseen, I need you to agree with Me.'"

God has put a destiny in you. He has put a purpose in you. Maybe you went the wrong way, did some stupid things, but the day you come back to God, that destiny is there waiting for you. It hasn't changed. It hasn't vanished. Don't listen to the lies of the devil. God's purpose for you hasn't changed. God has fulfilled it in you. So don't believe those lies anymore. Don't believe the devil anymore. Don't receive guilt and condemnation anymore. Christ has already done it in the unseen. Christ is the Redeemer and Restorer of time. He is the God of the impossible, and God does the impossible in our lives. We must get free of who we think God is.

God's purpose for you hasn't changed.
God has fulfilled it in you.

---

²³*Tell them therefore, thus says the Lord God: "I will lay this proverb to rest, and they shall no more use it as a proverb in Israel." But say to them, "The days are at hand, and the fulfillment of every vision.* (Ezekiel 12:23 NKJ)

Don't say, "God postpones. God gives setbacks." It's up to us not to agree with setbacks. We are to redeem the time for the days are evil. (Ephesians 5:16)

²*For He says, "In the time of My favor I heard you, and in the day of salvation I helped you." I tell you, now is the time of God's favor, now is the day of salvation.* (2 Corinthians 6:2 NIV)

God says, "The time is now. To-day!"

²⁵*But I the Lord will speak what I will, and it shall be fulfilled without delay. For in your days, you rebellious people, I will fulfill whatever I say, declares the Sovereign Lord.* (Ezekiel 12:25 NIV)

That's what God was saying to us about the building selling. "You rebellious people! Stop saying, 'The building isn't selling because it isn't God's timing.'" He was saying, "To-day is the day, now!" God spanked us good back then. God wants us to realize that we have to see it done now.

²⁷*Son of man, behold, they of the house of Israel say,*

"The vision that he seeth is for many days to come, and he prophesieth of the times that are far off." ²⁸*Therefore say unto them, "Thus saith the Lord GOD, 'There shall none of my words be prolonged any more, but the word which I have spoken shall be done,' saith the Lord GOD."* (Ezekiel 12:27-28 NKJ)

None of God's words are postponed. Call it done, see it done. The temple got done once they changed their confession and their mindset. We go from a vision, to a dream, to a movie and then it becomes visible. God's light illuminates the eyes of our imagination, floods our imagination with light until we experience the full revelation.

¹⁸*I pray that the light of God will illuminate the eyes of your imagination, flooding you with light, until you experience the full revelation of the hope of His calling—that is, the wealth of God's glorious inheritances that He finds in us, His holy ones!* (Ephesians 1:18 TPT)

Once we had confessed that the building was sold, saw it sold, agreed with God, "Now it's done," it sold by a total miracle within days! We are now in this beautiful building teaching God's Word, seeing peoples' lives changed, and seeing signs and wonders for many years.

This is what Jesus said to the disciples when He put them in the boat, *"...go over to the other side of the lake."* (Luke 8:22 NIV) Then Jesus went up to the mountain to pray. Half way to the other side of the lake, a storm came up, and it was a killer storm. It was an impossible storm to live through. (That's how bad it was).

Jesus, walking on the water, came along and rebuked the waves and the wind. That was a picture of the Word always working. He told them they were to go to the other side. God gave them the end before they started, then a storm came up against the Word of God before they could get to the finish.

It's the same with us. God tells us the end before we start, but it's up to us to speak, and see the end finished in the unseen. Call the end done in our prayer time. This is what faith looks like. *Fight the good fight of faith.* (1 Timothy 6:12 NIV)

"You are going to the other side. I gave you health, I gave you wealth, I gave you all the blessings. All the promises are yes and amen in Jesus. (2 Corinthians 1:20) Now see it in the unseen done."

"I gave you love, I gave you favor, I gave you success, I gave you your purpose. I already gave it all to you. Now see it done."

We can get going on our destiny, and then the enemy comes at us full force, the rug is pulled out from under us, and it becomes an impossibility. It's overwhelming, and too much! In the natural, it's impossible, but God is the God of the supernatural, the God of the impossible. His Word is all powerful to cut through and bring total success into each and every situation.

It's time for us to take on our authority, see the enemy under our feet, defeated and see ourselves on the other side, in the success of God's Word. The Word of God says we are to take on the perseverance of Christ. Christ already gave it to us. Take on the love of God, which was already poured out into our hearts by the Holy Spirit. (Romans 5:5)

¹Now faith is confidence in what we hope for and assurance about what we do not see. (Hebrew 11:1 NIV)

When you step into faith, you see the unseen done now. You have to see that. Faith is the proof, the evidence of things not yet seen in the natural.

⁹As the heavens are higher than the earth, so are My ways higher than your ways and My thoughts than your thoughts. ¹⁰*As the rain and the snow come down from heaven, and do not return to it without watering the earth and making it bud and flourish, so that it yields seed for the sower and bread for the eater,* ¹¹*so is My Word that goes out from My mouth: It will not return to Me empty, but will accomplish what I desire and achieve the purposes for which I sent it.* (Isaiah 55:9-11 NIV)

God is saying here, "I gave My Word. It can't fail, so take charge of the situation and call it done."

Show Us the Father
Chapter 4

Continuing on with New Covenant of Grace, it's what Christ has done, and in this Covenant, we go from blessing to blessing. The Old Covenant, which is obsolete, is what <u>we</u> do. Living under the Old Covenant, we go from one disaster to another, and we open ourselves to the curse. Jesus took the curse at the cross and paid the full price for our imperfections. He set us free to live a life of blessing, to experience one blessing after another.

It's very important to know that the Old Covenant is no more, and when the devil, who is a legalist, tries to get us under the Law, we need to respond to it as, "No, not at all, get behind me!" The Gospel is the death, burial, and resurrection of Christ, which takes us into the life of blessings and more blessings. This is the message of the cross, the power of God.

Looking at the Apostle Paul, who had a revelation of the Gospel of Grace, was called to the Gentiles, not the Jews, and the struggles he had convincing the Gentiles they were not to get under the Law. They never had the Law in the first place. Why were they so easily persuaded to get under the Law? It's the image they had inside of legalism and religion as they watched the religious people. It's the same today. It's the image we have on the inside of how we think religion should look when we come into the family of God.

Testimony

In my family, when I was growing up, we weren't church goers. I lived on a mink ranch in the country most of my life. Once in a while, I went to church if I could get a ride. As I grew up, I had an image on the inside of what Christianity should look like, and it was very religious. I was open to fall into legalism: what I had to do to earn God's love and favor and to get God to be happy with me. As legalism is, it was all about me and my performance. I went through the Bible to find all the don'ts so I wouldn't break one of them, just knowing God would be so happy with me. I fell right into a church where everything was sin except eating.

Praise God for the Holy Spirit Who showed me over time that Jesus was the only perfect One, and that I was free from my performance. Now it was all about Christ and His performance and my need to surrender to what Christ had done, the new Covenant of Grace. What a happy day that was, to go from one bad experience after another into a life of grace, living from blessing to blessing.

When you are under the Old Covenant of the Law, you are under the curse because if you break one law, you broke them all. No one is able to keep the Law, but Christ the perfect One. So in the Covenant of Grace, I'm under the works of Christ and all the promises are mine. The life of grace is knowing that I'm connected to Christ and His performance, and He did a complete work. It is finished.

With the way I looked at life and my attitude, it was, "Let me do it myself. I can do it!" I would plan it out in my mind, "I will do this, and I will do that, and it will be great."

Only when the project was finished, it was always way beneath my expectation and the yoke was too heavy and very disappointing. That wouldn't stop me because I thought, "Somehow, I will conquer this!"

Until I came into the revelation of grace, and by the Holy Spirit, I discovered that I can't do it, but Christ has already done it, and it's now Christ doing it through me. The projects God called me to do turned out way beyond my expectation. The yoke of Grace made it too easy, (because it was now Christ doing it through me) and I was overjoyed by the success. Christ in us the hope of glory. (Colossians 1:27)

Grace energizes us, revives us and implants within us passion to accomplish our destiny and all the excitement that goes along with the life of grace.

[13]God will continually revitalize you, implanting within you the passion to accomplish the good things you desire to do. (Philippians 12:13 TPT)

Grace fuels passion.

[9]My passion is to enlighten every person to this divine mystery. (Ephesians 3:9 TPT)

I was such a performer, such an earner,
and I thought I could actually do it myself.

This revelation of grace has set my whole life free. I was such a performer, such an earner, and I thought I could actually do it myself. In grace, we live in His abilities, His success, His faith, His love, His peace, His favor, His wealth, His power, His energy, His passion, etc. That's why it's so easy in grace. It's so successful, so full of passion, love and mercy.

Now grace doesn't make you lazy. I do more than I have ever done because it's supernatural. In this life of grace, we are children of God, born into the Family of God through our receiving Christ as our Savior. As sons of God, we can't earn our son ship, we are born into it and heirs of the promise.

⁷Therefore you are no longer a slave but a son, and if a son, then an heir of God through Christ. (Galatians 4:7 NKJ)

Now everything that is God's, is yours, through Christ. God looks at you through Christ. Praise God!

¹⁸The law, then, doesn't supersede the promise since the royal proclamation was given before the law. If that were the case, it would have nullified what God said to Abraham. We receive all the promises because of the Promised One—not because we keep the law! (Galatians 3:18 TPT)

³Every spiritual blessing in the heavenly realm has already been lavished upon us as a love gift from our wonderful heavenly Father, the Father of our Lord Jesus—all because He sees us wrapped into Christ. This is why we celebrate Him with all our hearts! (Ephesians 1:3 TPT)

We need to see this. When I sit down to pray, I realize that the Kingdom of God is in me. All that heaven contains has been already lavished upon me by Father God and that the Godhead dwells in me. So everything that's in the Kingdom is already in me. I'm an heir of it. I have it all in me, too much! Knowing this, believing it and connecting to it is what grace is all about. Knowing that Father God see's you in Christ, wrapped up in Christ, causes you to enter into rest in the generosity of Father God, a Father of too much. This causes us to celebrate Father God's goodness to us with all our hearts.

Now Paul is saying to them, "I pray over you the blessings of God."

³I pray over you a release of the blessings of God's underserved kindness and total well-being that flows from our Father-God and from the Lord Jesus. (Galatians 1:3 TPT)

I love this prayer because the first words Father God spoke over Adam and Eve were to bless them. The last words Jesus spoke over the disciples and His Church were to bless them.

²⁸Then God <u>blessed</u> them... (Genesis 1:28a NKJ)

⁵⁰...He lifted up His hands and <u>blessed</u> them. (Luke 24:50b NKJ)

⁵⁰Jesus led His disciples out to Bethany. He lifted His hands over them and blessed them in His love. ⁵¹While He was still speaking out words of love and blessing, He floated off the ground into the sky ascending into heaven before their very eyes. (Luke 24:50-51 TPT)

The heart desire of both God and Christ for us is to live from blessing to blessing. Of all the words God could have spoken, and the last words that Christ spoke, *blessed* - must be the most powerful word to us. *Blessed* mean wealth, health, peace, love, highly favored, joy and so much more.

So Paul was saying in His prayer over you that the wealth is already yours, the health is already yours, the peace, the love, favor, joy, and so much more is already yours. I'm standing in agreement with Father God's heart for you to live a life and a life more abundant so everything in your life is blessed.

¹⁴The Word became flesh and made His dwelling among us. We have seen His glory, the glory of the One and only Son, Who came from the Father, full of grace and truth. (John 1:14 NIV)

The Word, Christ Jesus, became a human being and dwelled with us. We have seen His glory. The word *glory* seems so mystical to me. Used here, it means power and character. We've seen His power of healing and miracles, but also His character of love and compassion for mankind. The Word, Christ Jesus, now dwells in us, and it is full of grace. We are now full of grace.

16From the fullness of His grace we have all received one blessing after another. (John 1:16 NIV84)

See! We are to go from blessing to blessing.

17For the law was given through Moses, but grace and truth came through Jesus Christ. (John 1:17 NKJV)

The Old Covenant that came through Moses is blessings and cursings, but the New Covenant that came through Christ Jesus is blessing and blessing.

4He's the Anointed Messiah Who offered Himself as the sacrifice for our sins! He has taken us out of this evil world system and set us free through our salvation, just as God desired. (Galatians 1:4 TPT)

Doesn't this excite you? It's not dependent on what you do, but on what Christ has already done through the Gospel of Grace (His death, burial, and resurrection.)

16 For God so loved the world that He gave His only begotten Son... (John 3:16 NKJ)

Paul was having problems with the false teachers who were trying to entice Christians to get back under the Law. And these Christians were leaving the life of grace and entering back into the bondage of the Mosaic Laws, from liberty to legalism.

Paul was bewildered at the instability of them sitting under his ministry. Not just once, but twice, leaving the Covenant of Grace and getting back under the legalistic teaching. Paul was shocked by the idea that anyone would twist or pervert the Gospel. What bothered Him most was they never even bothered to consult him, their spiritual father. They were, in effect, following strange teachings. It was like giving candy to a baby – polluted candy that is!

Paul was shocked by the idea that anyone would twist or pervert the Gospel.

---

⁶I am shocked over how quickly you have strayed away from the Anointed One Who called you to Himself by His loving mercy. I'm frankly astounded that you now embrace a distorted gospel! ⁷That is a fake "gospel" that is simply not true. There is only one gospel—the gospel of the Messiah! Yet you have allowed those who mingle law with grace to confuse you with lies. (Galatians 1:6-7 TPT)

¹⁸For if the inheritance depends on the Law, then it no longer depends on the promise; but God in His grace gave it to Abraham through a promise. (Galatians 3:18 NIV)

²¹I do not set aside the grace of God, for if righteousness could be gained through the law, Christ died for nothing!" (Galatians 2:21 NIV)

⁴You who are trying to be justified by the Law have been alienated from Christ; you have fallen away from grace. (Galatians 5:4 NIV)

⁶But now we are discharged from the Law and have terminated all intercourse with it, having died to what once restrained and held us captive. So now we serve not under [obedience to] the old code of written regulations, but [under obedience to the promptings] of the Spirit in newness [of life]. (Romans 7:6 AMPC)

We die to the law, and we enter into the New Covenant of what Christ has already done. That's the life for us because it's the abundant life.

In the New Covenant of Grace we entered into the life of the Holy Spirit. Now the Holy Spirit reveals to us Who the Father God truly is, free from the picture of the law. How we see our Father God will determine our trust in following Him, not in fear, but a knowing that He is a loving Father, and that He has already planned the best life for us, a life that's over the top, amazing!

[9]Jesus said to him, "Have I been with you so long, and yet you have not known Me, Philip? He who has seen Me has seen the Father; so how can you say, 'Show us the Father?'" (John 14:9 NKJ)

Philip says to Jesus, "Show us the Father," and Jesus says, "When you see Me, you have seen the Father."

[15]He (Jesus) is the image of the invisible God, the firstborn over all creation. (Colossians 1:15 NKJ)

Jesus is the image of the invisible God.

Jesus is the image of the invisible God. As we look at the Gospel, and see the behavior of Jesus, we get to know our Father God and His heart for mankind. We see His loving, caring heart towards them. We need to shake off the image that religion has painted in our hearts that keeps us in fear of God as though He is an abusive Father.

As the Holy Spirit was revealing to me the life of Jesus, He was painting a new and true picture of the Father God. Think about the woman at the well in the Gospel of John.

⁶Now Jacob's well was there. Jesus therefore, being wearied from His journey, sat thus by the well. It was about the sixth hour.

⁷A woman of Samaria came to draw water. Jesus said to her,

"Give Me a drink." ⁸For His disciples had gone away into the city to buy food.

⁹Then the woman of Samaria said to Him,

"How is it that You, being a Jew, ask a drink from me, a Samaritan woman?" For Jews have no dealings with Samaritans.

¹⁰Jesus answered and said to her,

"If you knew the gift of God, and Who it is Who says to you, 'Give Me a drink,' you would have asked Him, and He would have given you living water."

¹¹The woman said to Him, "Sir, You have nothing to draw with, and the well is deep. Where then do You get that living water? ¹²Are You greater than our father Jacob, who gave us the well, and drank from it himself, as well as his sons and his livestock?"

¹³Jesus answered and said to her, "Whoever drinks of this water will thirst again, ¹⁴but whoever drinks of the water that I shall give him will never thirst. But the water that I shall give him will become in him a fountain of water springing up into everlasting life."

¹⁵ The woman said to Him,

"Sir, give me this water, that I may not thirst, nor come here to draw."

¹⁶ Jesus said to her,

"Go, call your husband, and come here."

¹⁷ The woman answered and said,

"I have no husband."

Jesus said to her,

"You have well said, 'I have no husband,' ¹⁸*for you have had five husbands, and the one whom you now have is not your husband; in that you spoke truly."*

¹⁹*The woman said to Him,*

"Sir, I perceive that You are a prophet. ²⁰*Our fathers worshiped on this mountain, and you Jews say that in Jerusalem is the place where one ought to worship."*

²¹*Jesus said to her,*

"Woman, believe Me, the hour is coming when you will neither on this mountain, nor in Jerusalem, worship the Father. (John 4:6-21 NKJ)

Jesus' ministry was only three and one-half years. Yet one morning in that short time on earth, He awoke to reveal to us the heart of Father God, Who led Him that day to Samaria.

Now the Samaritans were hated by the Jews, but Jesus went there to meet with a woman. She was a woman who was despised by religion. She had been married five times and was now living with a man.

Father God saw her heart and her captivity with His love full of mercy, and He sent Jesus to deliver her.

Jesus sat there in the heat of the day waiting for her. Why! Father God saw her heart and her captivity. And in His love that is full of mercy, He sent Jesus to deliver her. She was a despised woman in the eyes of mankind but not to Father God. Man looks at the outward appearance, the outward behavior, but God looks at the heart.

In religion men didn't talk to women especially a woman like her. Father God, through Jesus, was showing her the way to her freedom in a life with Father God, the New Covenant. Father God saw her as precious, valuable and opened His arms to receive her.

Of course God hates sin, but He loves the sinner. Just think of those times when the presence of Father God came on you, and the value you felt at that moment. This is what was happening to this woman at the well. Those times are truly life-changing moments. As we see in this Scripture, this was a life-changing moment for her, and she had to go tell the whole town. When we experience those times with the Father God, we are never the same.

Think of the woman caught in adultery. The religious group brought her to Jesus and with their hearts full of judgement, said,

⁴"Teacher, this woman was caught in the act of adultery. ⁵In the Law Moses commanded us to stone such women. Now what do you say?" (John 8:4-5 NIV)

As we see the heart of the Father, through Jesus, full of mercy and love for her, a Father Who wants to hold her and say,

"It's going to be alright. I love you! You are valuable to Me. I've sent My Son for you to deliver you from this captivity. I am your Father God, your Defender and your Protector."

Jesus hated the ways of the religious group because they portrayed Father God as an unloving father, having no mercy and a heart waiting for us to blow it so He can abuse us.

Religion attacks the character of our Father God. After Jesus wrote in the sand, (He was her Defender) Jesus looked at her and said,

¹⁰"Woman, where are they? Has no one condemned you?"

[11]"No one, sir, " she said. (John 8:10-11 NIV)

And Jesus, showing her the Father's heart for her, said,

[11] "Then neither do I condemn you...go now and leave your life of sin. " (John 8:11 NIV)

She, at that moment, was set free of her captivity of sin by the very powerful words of Jesus.

Jesus is Grace.

Jesus was the picture of grace. Jesus is grace, and what does grace do? It gives us the power and ability to be totally free from addictions, sin, and captivity. Grace gives us the ability to say no to sin. Grace is a mentor, a teacher, a trainer in our lives. Grace

[12]...teaches us to say "No" to ungodliness and worldly passions, and to live self-controlled, upright and godly lives in this present age. (Titus 2:12 NIV)

Grace came to this earth through Christ Jesus to paint the right picture in us of what the New Covenant of Grace would look like. The Gospel tells us that Jesus only spoke the Father's words and only did what He saw the Father do. When we see Jesus in the Gospels we see the Father God being displayed before us.

[19]"Very truly I tell you, the Son can do nothing by Himself; He can do only what He sees His Father doing, because whatever the Father does the Son also does. (John 5:19b NIV)

Think about when Jesus went to the home of the Pharisees, and the woman who was living a sinful life showed up. When she saw Jesus, she immediately kneeled before Him with a heart to honor Him as her Savior Who could save her from her life of sin. She began to kiss His feet, wash them with her tears and wipe them with her hair. Then she anointed his feet with costly oil. She was crying out for help.

39 When the Pharisee who had invited Him saw this, he said to himself, "If this man were a prophet, he would know who is touching him and what kind of woman she is—that she is a sinner." (Luke 7:39 NIV)

This Pharisee, and the religious group in his home, had nothing but judgement, condemnation, guilt, and shame for her. Jesus, knowing his thoughts, went on to say to the Pharisees,

44 "I came into your house. You did not give me any water for My feet, but she wet My feet with her tears and wiped them with her hair. 45 You did not give me a kiss, but this woman, from the time I entered, has not stopped kissing my feet. 46 You did not put oil on my head, but she has poured perfume on my feet. 47 Therefore, I tell you, her many sins have been forgiven—as her great love has shown. But whoever has been forgiven little loves little."

48 Then Jesus said to her, "Your sins are forgiven."

49 The other guests began to say among themselves, "Who is this who even forgives sins?"

50 Jesus said to the woman, "Your faith has saved you; go in peace."

Oh my goodness! Jesus is again revealing to us the very loving, merciful, caring heart of the Father God, a heart overflowing with love for us, His precious children. The Word says

13 If you then, though you are evil, know how to give good gifts to your children, how much more will your Father in heaven give the Holy Spirit to those who ask Him! (Luke 11:13 NIV)

How about Zacchaeus, the worst of sinners!

¹Jesus entered Jericho and was passing through. ²A man was there by the name of Zacchaeus; he was a chief tax collector and was wealthy. ³He wanted to see who Jesus was, but because he was short he could not see over the crowd. ⁴So he ran ahead and climbed a sycamore-fig tree to see him, since Jesus was coming that way.

⁵When Jesus reached the spot, He looked up and said to him, "Zacchaeus, come down immediately. I must stay at your house today." ⁶So he came down at once and welcomed him gladly. (Luke 19:1-6 NIV)

Out of all of the people following Jesus, He chooses Zacchaeus' house. It's again showing us in the Gospels that God looks at the heart of man and not the outward appearance. Jesus, walking the earth and touching lives of those who are caught up in sin and addictions and can in no way help themselves...but Jesus.

Oh, that we would be people
who look beyond behavior and see the heart!

Oh, that we would be people who look beyond behavior and see the heart! God wants mercy instead of sacrifice, (Matthew 9:13) a heart of love and compassion for people and to know Jesus has the answer for them, an answer of freedom from their captivity and not judgement.

Jesus chose Zacchaeus' house and Zacchaeus chose a new life of freedom because Jesus gave him value and acceptance. God wants us to get the right image of Who He really is.

51

Look at Rahab, a chief prostitute, in the Old Testament Book of Joshua. She had a heart that was crying out for God. She saved the lives of the two spies, and the spies then saved her life and her family.

When you give to God, He always multiplies your return. Rahab, a prostitute, not a Jew, marries Salmon and becomes the great, great grandmother of King David and she is in the bloodline of Jesus! (Matthew 1:5)

We are seeing God as He really is, a merciful, loving and generous Father, Who loves to forgive much and doesn't remember our past.

Look at Judah's daughter-in-law, Tamar. (Genesis 38) She deceives Judah, becomes pregnant by him and has twins. Tamar and one of her twins ends up in the bloodline of Jesus.

This is Bible. For God hates sin but loves the sinner. We need to let these examples get into our hearts and change us to have the right picture of Father God.

The Word of God states that Jesus became like us in all points, tempted as we are, yet was without sin, a compassionate, merciful, faithful High Priest Who sympathizes with our weaknesses. (Hebrews 2:17, 4:15) The law is judgmental when it's based on what we can do, but grace is merciful and loving because it's based on what Christ has done.

Jesus at the cross took the sins of the world upon Himself and when the punishment of it all fell on Him, He said,

[24] *"Father, forgive them, for they know not what they do."* (Luke 23:24)

Jesus set us free by His works to have His power to live free from the power of addictions, selfishness, generational curses and sin, to live an abundant, blessed life.

[10]I have come that they may have life, and that they may have it more abundantly. (John 10:10b NKJ)

Jesus is saying, "My desire is to give you everything in abundance, more than you expect—life in its fullness until you overflow!"

These are examples for you to connect to the unconditional love of Father God for you. When you come to Father God, He already made a way of escape for you. It's not what religion says who the Father God is. It's not what legalism says who the Father God is, but it's Who Jesus says He is. For when you see Jesus, you see the Father.

He's a Father Who understands
our wrong decisions in life and makes a way of escape.

Jesus was consumed with compassion for the sick and hurting. He delivered people from their captivity. He loved unconditionally. He adored and valued people with all His heart for He gave it all so we could have eternal life and live life and have life more abundant, being blessed beyond blessing.

[3]The Son is the radiance of God's glory and the exact representation of His being, sustaining all things by His powerful word. (Hebrew 1:3a NIV)

Glory in that verse means "power and character." Jesus, the exact representation of Father God, shows us a Father full of mercy, compassion, unconditional love, favor, value, grace, joy, and blessings. He's a Father Who saved Rahab, the prostitute, and Tamar, Judah's daughter-in-law. He's a Father Who understands our prisons, our addictions, our helplessness and He cares. He's a Father Who understands our wrong decisions in life and makes a way of escape. That's Who our Father God is.

³Every spiritual blessing in the heavenly realm has already been lavished upon us as a love gift from our wonderful heavenly Father, the Father of our Lord Jesus—all because He sees us wrapped into Christ. This is why we celebrate Him with all our hearts! (Ephesians 1:3 TPT)

We need to reframe the way we see our Father God by the words we say and by the thoughts we think.

Grace is an Energy, a Force, a Power
Chapter 5

The Apostle Paul was called to the Gentiles to bring the Word of Grace. In each of his writings by the Holy Spirit, he was dealing with the Gentiles who had come into the Gospel of Grace and then had gotten back under the Law of Moses. This is the picture they had within, and many times this is the very picture we have inside of us when we come into our personal relationship with Jesus as our Lord and Savior. In each of the writings, the Apostle Paul is giving them a new picture, a right picture of how the Gospel of Grace looks. What we see inside is what we believe, and what we see inside is how we will live. The image of Father God on the inside will determine the outcome of our life.

The image of Father God on the inside
will determine the outcome of our life.

We need to get free of religious, legalistic behavior and belief systems about our Father God that will harm our walk and the way we behave.

Jesus was upset with the religious group in His time because they were attacking the character of God. They were not painting a loving, caring, giving Father but a false image of a heavy task master, a policeman of the universe or a stern, abusive boss.

Think of the woman with the issue of blood. She came to Jesus in desperation, penniless, and sick for many years to touch the hem of His garment. As she touched Him, she was instantly healed. By law, she was forbidden to be in the crowd, and breaking this law meant being stoned to death, but Jesus, a picture of Father God, said,

45 *"Who touched Me?"*

When they all denied it, Peter said,

"Master, the people are crowding and pressing against You."

46 *But Jesus said,*

"Someone touched Me; I know that power has gone out from Me."

47 *Then the woman, seeing that she could not go unnoticed, came trembling and fell at His feet. In the presence of all the people, she told why she had touched Him and how she had been instantly healed.* 48 *Then He said to her,*

"Daughter, your faith has healed you. Go in peace." (Luke 8:45-48 NIV)

Jesus didn't condemn her, shame her or have her stoned to death, but loved her and healed her.

We must embrace Father God by what Christ revealed to us about our Father.

Jairus is another example in which we can see the Father's heart through Jesus.

22 *Then one of the synagogue leaders, named Jairus, came, and when he saw Jesus, he fell at his feet.* 23 *He pleaded earnestly with Him,*

"My little daughter is dying. Please come and put Your hands on her so that she will be healed and live."

24 *So Jesus went with him.* (Mark 5:22-24 NIV)

35 *While Jesus was still speaking, some people came from the house of Jairus, the synagogue leader.*

"Your daughter is dead," they said. "Why bother the teacher anymore?"

³⁶*Overhearing what they said, Jesus told him,*
"Don't be afraid; just believe."

³⁷*He did not let anyone follow Him except Peter, James and John the brother of James.* ³⁸*When they came to the home of the synagogue leader, Jesus saw a commotion, with people crying and wailing loudly.* ³⁹*He went in and said to them,*

"Why all this commotion and wailing? The child is not dead but asleep."

⁴⁰*But they laughed at Him. After He put them all out, He took the child's father and mother and the disciples who were with Him, and went in where the child was.* ⁴¹*He took her by the hand and said to her,*

"Talitha koum!" (which means "Little girl, I say to you, get up!").

⁴²*Immediately the girl stood up and began to walk around (she was twelve years old).* (Mark 5:35-42 NIV)

Do you see Father God as a heavy task master?

Jesus went right to Jairus' home and raised his daughter from the dead! Here again, Jesus is portraying Father God to us as an all-powerful, loving, caring Father Who is full of mercy.

Do you see Father God as a heavy task master? Do you believe that His love for you is based on your service, your performance, that you must earn His love, His blessings, His mercy or His favor? Jesus answers this question in the sixth chapter of John.

²⁸*Then they asked Him,*
"What must <u>we do</u> to do the works God requires?"
²⁹*Jesus answered,*

"The work of God is this: to <u>believe</u> in the One He has sent." (John 6:28-29 NIV)

Jesus said the works we must do is to *"believe in the One He has sent."*

Testimony

I was one of those over-achievers in life. In high school, I had to work to get the best grades, be the best cheerleader, be in every club and be the best at everything. In college and nursing school, I worked hard to be the best. I came into the Kingdom of God, and I fell right into being an over-achiever. Now I had to earn God's love and acceptance. My image of God on the inside was that of a heavy task master. It was all about what I could do and not about what Christ had done for me. I never could get to the level I was expecting in my life, but I never quit. I just kept trying and trying over and over again. Thank God for the Holy Spirit Who set me free by giving me a revelation of grace!

It was all about what I could do and not about what Christ had done for me.

The revelation of grace isn't us coming to God to tell Him what we are going to do. Rather, it's us going to God to find out what He has already done. Then we can take what's in the invisible (in God's heart) and bring it into the visible.

[10]For we are His workmanship, created in Christ Jesus for good works, which God prepared beforehand that we should walk in them. (Ephesians 2:10 NKJ)

So, in God's plan, we are always successful, and we always win as we take on God's heart for us. This is His grace and where it carries us, we are able to enter His rest.

¹⁰*...for anyone who enters God's rest also rests from their works, just as God did from His.* (Hebrews 4:10 NIV)

Now, in grace, we step into <u>His love</u>. We step into <u>His faith</u>. We step into <u>His favor</u>. We step into <u>His everything</u>! It's His works and not ours.

Testimony

Thirty years ago I woke up one day to frozen shoulders. This is where calcium builds up in the shoulders, and it's extremely painful to move your arms. Now the only way to be free from this in the natural is to have surgery on both shoulders. But I took authority over my body and commanded my shoulder bones to return to normal and the frozen shoulder to be gone! Within six months my shoulders were back to normal and have been that way for over 30 years now.

One day my right thumb became very painful to move, and I could barely use it. The strength in my thumb was completely gone. Again, I took authority over the thumb pain and immobility, and again, within six months, the thumb was back to normal.

I found out later that in my family history, the tendon shortens over time and needs to be operated on to correct it. Well, God totally fixed it without surgery.

What I'm saying here is that in your new-found life in Christ Jesus, you reframe your world by what Christ says in His Word, and not by what your body says. This takes time.

The Word of God is a seed.

[11] *"This is the meaning of the parable: The seed is the word of God.* (Luke 8:11 NIV)

There's seed, and then there's time.

[22] *"As long as the earth endures, seed-time and harvest...* (Genesis 8:22 NIV)

Seedtime is hyphenated, *seed-time,* which indicates it is two separate words: *seed* and *time.* We plant the *seed,* the Word of God. Then, it's in the *time* where the battle is. That's where we reframe our situation to match what God's Word says. (Our agreement with the seed.) In the unseen is where God reveals His plan to us so we can connect our thoughts to His plan followed by our words of agreement.

We aren't trying to get it. We already got it! We connect to the seed of God's Word to get rid of the lie (the current situation) and then comes the harvest.

We must *fight the good fight of faith* (1 Timothy 6:12) because *time* is the battle. There is always a storm. There is always the impossible. There's always that negative thought. The Word says that the enemy comes to steal the seed and to persecute you because of the seed. (Mark 4:15, 17) What I'm saying, is it takes the supernatural grace of God that gives you the power to hold onto the seed that produces the harvest.

In the Kingdom of His grace, you find rest for your soul because it always ends up greater than you expected. Wow! You're not disappointed with the harvest because it's greater than you expected. It's beyond your greatest dream, your wildest imagination! Now you are overwhelmed by His goodness.

[20]*Never doubt God's mighty power to work in you and accomplish all this. He will achieve infinitely more than your greatest request, your most unbelievable dream, and exceed your wildest imagination! He will outdo them all, for His*

miraculous power constantly energizes you. (Ephesians 3:20 TPT)

God will outdo every seed because of the power that is working in you. We need to be sure that we keep our words and thoughts in agreement with God and stay in agreement with what He has already done.

¹³God will continually revitalize you, implanting within you the passion to do what pleases Him. (Philippians 2:13 TPT)

When we connect to the Word of God, let His Word cover us with His grace, it implants within us the passion we need to accomplish the good things we desire to do.

²May God Himself, the heavenly Father of our Lord Jesus Christ, release grace over you... (Ephesians 1:2 TPT)

⁶...so that His tremendous love that cascades over us would glorify His grace... (Ephesians 1:6 TPT)

In grace, it's not us trying to keep the passion going.

In grace it's not us trying to keep the passion going. It's not us trying to keep the life going, the joy, the love, the victory. No, it's grace itself that does the work. We are only entering the rest of grace. In grace we are continually revitalized. The passion is grace fired up in you to accomplish the God thing.

¹²...I run with passion into His abundance so that I may reach the purpose that Jesus Christ has called me to fulfill and wants me to discover. ¹³I don't depend on my own strength to accomplish this... (Philippians 3:12-13 TPT)

Grace gives us the passion to run into everything in the Kingdom so we may reach the destiny God has for us. It's not going to be with our strength but the supernatural strength of grace.

⁹My passion is to enlighten every person to this divine mystery. (Ephesians 3:9 TPT)

What fuels your passion? What fires you up and gives you energy? It's grace! It's resting in Father God's sufficiency and not your own.

The grace life depends upon letting Christ's life live in you and through you. Grace is not what you do, but what Christ has done.

Let Christ's life, His power, His love, His behavior, His passion, and His sufficiency flow through you that others might see the heart of the Father through you.

In a life of grace, you are free to receive all the blessings working for you. In a life driven by law, (what you can do) the curse is working against you. We are in a New Covenant of what Christ has already done. The Old Covenant is now obsolete.

¹³In speaking of the New Covenant, He makes the first one obsolete. (Hebrews 8:13 ESV)

If we go back under the law, the curse rules over our lives because if we break one of the laws, we broke them all.

¹⁰For whoever keeps the whole law and yet stumbles at just one point is guilty of breaking it all. (James 2:10 NIV)

The law is good, it's holy, but we are imperfect beings who cannot keep the law. Christ was the only One Who could keep the law. Now we are in the New Covenant under His works, clothed in Him.

Under the law, we are earners, and under grace, we become receivers. We believe in the works of Christ, His promises to us, we surrender to them, and we receive them. Following these steps, the promises become flesh and dwell among us. These promises are able to flow through us and touch the lives of others.

Grace is an energy, it's a force, and it's a power. Stepping into the power of grace, we let what He has done become a reality in our lives and the lives of others. We are actually partakers of His divine nature.

²And do not be conformed to this world, but be transformed by the renewing of your mind, that you may prove what is that good and acceptable and perfect will of God. (Romans 12:2 NKJ)

Conformed to this world means getting under our good works. It's what we can do in our own self-effort. But being *transformed* means to make that paradigm shift into what Christ has already done. It's depending on His works to flow through us and produce after its kind.

---

*Their faith fastened onto their promises
and pulled them into reality.*

How do we accomplish this? Changing our thoughts to think God thoughts, creating new ruts in our minds.

³Fix your heart on the promises of God and you will be secure, feasting on His faithfulness. (Psalm 37:3 TPT)

³³Their faith fastened onto their promises and pulled them into reality. (Hebrews 11:33 TPT)

We don't think on the negative, the curse, but we think on what God says, on the positive, on the blessings, knowing that all the blessings of Abraham are ours. We bring our thoughts into agreement with what God is saying. By right thoughts, which are God's thoughts, we can then prove what

God's will is for us. (Romans 12:2) This is how we step into God's destiny for us. It starts with the right thoughts.

⁶And they have fastened Your Word firmly to their hearts. (John 17:6 TPT)

⁸They have received Your words and carry them in their hearts. (John 17:8 TPT)

God has already accomplished His destiny for me in the unseen. I'm now able to receive it to work through me because of right thinking. Praise God! So transforming my mind is not me trying to earn my destiny, being an earner, but me receiving what He has already done in the unseen and letting it live through me. I'm not trying to get healthy. I'm already healthy. I'm not trying to be successful. I'm already successful. I'm not trying to get wealthy. I'm already wealthy. I'm not trying to get loving. I'm already loving, full of His divine nature.

¹¹So then we must give our all and be eager to experience this faith-rest life, so that no one falls short by following the same pattern of doubt and unbelief. (Hebrews 4:11 TPT)

We need to continue on more with the image of Father God. As I mentioned earlier, how I see Father God on the inside will determine my future, the outcome of my life. Jesus prayed,

⁶"Father, I have manifested Who You really are and I have revealed You to the men and women that You gave to Me. (John 17:6 TPT)

Jesus said, "*Anyone who has seen Me, has seen the Father.*" (John 14:9 NIV) The Word says that Jesus is the image of the invisible Father God, the exact representation of our Father God. (Hebrews 1:3)

When we read the Gospels, we see the Father God. A Father Who is full of blessings, full of compassion, Who healed the sick, and raised the dead. A Father God Who set the sinner free from shame, condemnation or guilt. A Father Who gave it all so we could be free of the devil and live an overwhelmingly-blessed life. A Father Who redeemed us to be His precious children. Such love He lavished on us. This is the Father God Who Jesus painted for us to see.

Jesus was unhappy with the religious crowd because they were attacking the very character of God. They were painting a picture in the hearts of the people that Father God is a stern Father, Who is abusive with His children. Jesus was not happy with the way they were portraying God and the way they were treating the people. Isn't that how we are when someone attacks the character of someone we love?

If we see the image of Father God as a heavy task master, then it's all about our service. Will He love me? Will He be pleased with me? Will He reward me? With this incorrect image, I have to perform to get Father God's love and approval.

Jesus already performed for us! He already pleased the Father by His believing. He already earned the blessings for us. Again, all we have to do now is believe. Jesus said,

[29] *"The work of God is this: to believe in the One He has sent."* (John 6:29 NIV)

We are to believe, and yet Jesus even provided that for us! Jesus is the beginner of our faith.

Let's attack another wrong image of the Father God that we could be carrying on the inside of us. It's the image of Father God as the moral policeman of the universe. What do I mean by that? He is waiting for us to fail or make a mistake at any moment to punish us or to put sickness or poverty or storms on us to make us better. It's the image of a Father God Who kills us because He needs us in heaven.

18There is no fear in love. But perfect love drives out fear, because fear has to do with punishment. The one who fears is not made perfect in love. (I John 4:18 NIV)

15For the law provokes punishment, and where no law exists there cannot be a violation of the law. 16The promise depends on faith so that it can be experienced as a grace gift, and now it extends to all the descendants of Abraham. (Romans 4:15-16 TPT)

10The thief does not come except to steal, and to kill, and to destroy. I (Jesus) have come that they may have life, and that they may have it more abundantly. (John 10:10 NKJ)

Satan is a legalist, and he comes to steal, to kill and to destroy. Satan puts us into a place of condemnation, guilt and shame. But Jesus came to give us life and not just life, but life more abundantly, a life of too much!

Our loving Father goes way beyond what we expect, way beyond our most unbelievable dreams and wildest imagination!

10...everything in abundance, more than you expect — life in its fullness until you overflow. (John 10:10 TPT)

This is the true heart of the Father for us. Our loving Father goes way beyond what we expect, way beyond our most unbelievable dreams and our wildest imagination! God outdoes them all. Wow!

Our Father God doesn't hold our sins against us nor remember them anymore.

6And in this same way David speaks of the blessing on the one to whom God credits righteousness apart from works:

[7]*"Blessed and happy and favored are those whose lawless acts have been forgiven, and whose sins have been covered up and completely buried.* [8]*Blessed and happy and favored is the man whose sin the Lord will not take into account nor charge against him."* (Romans 4:6-8 AMP)

This is grace! Praise God!

Let's talk about King David.

[25]*David said about him:*

"I saw the Lord always before me. Because He is at my right hand, I will not be shaken. [26]*Therefore my heart is glad and my tongue rejoices; my body also will rest in hope,* [27]*because You will not abandon me to the realm of the dead, You will not let your holy one see decay.* [28]*You have made known to me the paths of life; You will fill me with joy in Your presence."*

[29]*"Fellow Israelites, I can tell you confidently that the patriarch David died and was buried, and his tomb is here to this day.* [30]*But he was a prophet and knew that God had promised him on oath that he would place one of his descendants on his throne.* [31]*Seeing what was to come, he spoke of the resurrection of the Messiah, that he was not abandoned to the realm of the dead, nor did His body see decay."* (Acts 2:25-31 NIV)

This Scripture tells us that King David saw the death, burial and resurrection of Christ Jesus in His lifetime. King David saw the New Covenant of Grace. Because God is the Alpha and Omega, the Beginning and the End, He began, and then He finished and then He began. So, Father God opened to King David the future of Christ's death, burial, and resurrection, and King David believed and received the Covenant of Grace.

King David had an affair with Bathsheba, found out he had impregnated her, had her husband killed and then married her. We see He committed one sin after another. The prophet, Nathan, came to King David and brought King David's sin out into the open. Nathan prophesied that the child would die. The child did die and David went into repentance.

After King David repented, He went into Bathsheba and she became pregnant and along came King Solomon. King Solomon was one of the greatest kings of all. (See 2 Samuel 11 and 12.)

23King Solomon was greater in riches and wisdom than all the other kings of the earth. (1 Kings 10:23 NIV)

Now grace is not a license to sin. Grace gives us the power and ability to <u>not</u> sin, (Titus 2:12) but this is a picture of grace when we repent. King Solomon is still today recorded as the richest king throughout history.

The Bible says that God visited Solomon, and that he built the temple. In all of this, Solomon wasn't in line to be king – under the law. The older brother was to be the king under the law, but God instead chose Solomon to be king. Now this is a picture of Father God and His redemptive power for us. This is a picture of grace: King Solomon being born to King David and Bathsheba. We can't understand this, but this is grace. Stop and meditate on this picture. The older brother was to become king but in grace, Solomon was chosen. (1 Kings 1:5-40 NKJ)

7Blessed and happy and favored are those whose lawless acts have been forgiven, and whose sins have been covered up and completely buried. 8Blessed and happy and favored is the man whose sin the Lord will not take into account nor charge against him. (Romans 4:7-8 AMP)

Oh my goodness! Did you read that? King David said this. Praise God! King David was saying, "Do you know this in your heart? Do you know that God doesn't hold your sins against you?"

Testimony

This is very interesting in my own life. I was called to help my husband build Living Word Bible Church, and I had never built a church before. So no matter how hard we tried to do everything perfect, we are imperfect beings. When I would miss the mark in building the church, I would be full of condemnation and shame.

God doesn't hold our imperfections against us, but I was holding my imperfections against myself. (I had a wrong image of Father God.) Because my belief system was all messed up, every time something would happen in this situation, I would blame myself,

"See, you caused this!"

One day I was walking down the hall of the church, and I heard myself say,

"How long do I have to pay for this?"

And the Holy Spirit spoke and said to me,

"As long as you believe that way, you will keep reaping that."

What? In grace, God sets us free from religious beliefs. God began to work on me, and it took almost a year to make the paradigm shift to believe that God doesn't hold our sins against us. Once we admit we failed and give it to God, He produces a King Solomon in our life. I mean He turns it into a supernatural event that is better than we ever expected!

28 And we know that all things work together for good to those who love God, to those who are the called according to His purpose. (Romans 8:28 NKJ)

Our Father God's blessings aren't a result of our faithfulness, but because of our Father God's faithfulness. Father God doesn't bless us because of how wonderful we are, but because of how wonderful Father God is!

We can miss the mark and keep believing for a wrong harvest because we have the incorrect image of God in our hearts. God is not the moral policeman of the universe. We get what we believe for. We need to believe for a crop failure, and give it to God. Then watch our Father God turn it into good.

Father God already knows we are imperfect beings, and that is why He sent Jesus to rescue us from ourselves. Father God desires to draw us to Himself and give us a life of blessings free from condemnation and guilt.

We must get this paradigm shift into our minds. It's not about what we do but about what He has done.

34 Jesus said, "Father, forgive them, for they do not know what they are doing." (Luke 23:34 NIV)

When I, over the years, would read those scriptures, I always thought it was about what was happening at that moment. They had mocked Him, beaten Him, put the crown of thorns on His head, and nailed Him to the cross. But then God gave me a revelation of what Christ was really saying here: At the cross, Jesus took all the sins of the world, the past sins, the sins right then, and the future sins of the world. Jesus, at the cross, took all the punishment for those sins, and paid it in full. When it was completed, then

34 Jesus said, "Father, forgive them, for they do not know what they are doing." (Luke 23:34 NIV)

Oh, my gosh! Do you see the magnitude of what He was saying there? Your past, present, and future sins are all paid in full with all the punishment needed. This means that all your sins are blotted out, wiped away, and remembered no more. Now think about this: Jesus was made like us in all things and tempted like us in everything yet was without sin so He could be a merciful, faithful High Priest.

[17]Therefore, in all things He had to be made like His brethren, that He might be a merciful and faithful High Priest in things pertaining to God, to make propitiation for the sins of the people. [18]For in that He Himself has suffered, being tempted, He is able to aid those who are tempted. (Hebrews 2:17-18 NKJ)

[15]For we do not have a High Priest Who cannot sympathize with our weaknesses, but was in all points tempted as we are, yet without sin. (Hebrews 4:15 NKJ)

It takes grace to open our eyes to the magnitude of this forgiveness.

Because He is our merciful and faithful High Priest, Jesus understands that we don't know what we are doing when we sin. What did Jesus say in Luke 23:34?

"They don't know what they are doing."

Can we really comprehend that? It takes grace to open our eyes to the magnitude of this forgiveness. If we are forgiven by the works of Jesus on the cross and our sins are blotted out, erased, they can't be held against us. We've been set free! Now take on your freedom. God is not demanding perfection.

We don't see how we hurt others by our sin. We don't see how we hurt the Father God. Jesus said that we don't know what we are doing. Jesus understood that about us.

Now when I came into the born-again experience I wanted to do everything right. Of course, that's a right heart, except I thought I really could. But we can't. Our love is conditional. Jesus said,

34As I have loved you, so you must love one another. (John 13:34 NIV)

Well, we can't! We need His love. It's the same with forgiveness. I wanted to forgive. Oh, how I wanted to, but I couldn't. I tried everything until I admitted that I couldn't. I needed His forgiveness. Jesus is the Forgiver. Once I let go and let Jesus be the Forgiver, I was set free.

In grace it's all about Him. Jesus already forgave their past, present, and future sins. This is amazing! This kind of forgiveness is a picture of grace in our lives. Every blessing finds its source in this grace. Christ is our faith, our trust, Christ is our love, our behavior, our voice, our strength. As a matter of fact, He is our everything!

17And since we are His true children, we qualify to share all His treasures, for indeed, we are heirs of God Himself. And since we are joined to Christ, we also inherit all that He is and all that He has. (Romans 8:17 TPT)

We inherit all that He is. That's why He is the Forgiver. And all that God has is ours. He shares it all with us.

In Christ, We Always Win
Chapter 6

Let's continue on our journey of discovering the true heart of our Father God, allowing the life of Jesus to reveal to us the true image of God. He's a Father Who has loved us unconditionally, is over-the-top generous to us, and a merciful Father Who has given us all things in Christ Jesus. We are letting go of the image of a heavy task master father who only loves us if we perform.

In the New Covenant, we see Father God always loves us unconditionally based on Jesus' performance and the blessings are ours in Christ Jesus. The blessings are working for us. Father God loves you because you exist!

Father God loves you because you exist!

We are changing our image of Father God to the true image. We are saying no to the image we have of Him being the moral policeman of the universe who is looking for our failures so He can punish us, who brings sickness, poverty, and storms in our lives to make us better.

These are the images that religion has portrayed to us. The true image of Father God is a Father Who doesn't hold our sins against us. Jesus shows us the true nature of our Father God as He walked this earth and healed the sick, raised the dead, cried with the hurting, set the sinner free, never condemned, shamed, but loved everyone unconditionally.

Legalism depicts Father God as a stern, abusive father, not a loving father, but a father who is harsh, demanding, brutal at times, and distant. And whatever we do, it's never

73

good enough. In this image of our Abba Father there is no room to enjoy life because we are never good enough.

Well, we are never good enough in our own good works, but we are not in our good works when we are in grace. We are in Jesus' good works. Father God sees us wrapped in Christ, accepted in the beloved.

[3]He sees us wrapped into Christ. This is why we celebrate Him with all our hearts! (Ephesians 1:3 TPT)

[1]See what great love the Father has lavished on us, that we should be called children of God! And that is what we are! (1 John 3:1 NIV)

Such love that Father God lavished on us that we should be called children of God!

What was Jesus showing us about our Father God in the Parable of the Prodigal Son? As we look at Luke 15:11-28, we see the oldest son as a picture of religious believers and legalism. The younger son is a picture of grace. Now we know grace is not a license to sin, but grace gives us the power and ability to be free from sin.

[11]For the grace of God has appeared that offers salvation to all people. [12]It teaches us to say "No" to ungodliness and worldly passions, and to live self-controlled, upright and godly lives in this present age. (Titus 2:11-12 NIV)

While we are in the midst of sin, Father God still loves us unconditionally with mercy, not judgment, with total forgiveness and restoration in His heart for us.

So the younger son asked for his inheritance while his father was living, and He got it. He moved far away from the father and squandered all the wealth with wild living and prostitutes. A famine hit the town, and this son is now with the pigs, at the bottom, starving. So he decides to go to the father with a heart of repentance. The son is filled up with condemnation, guilt, and shame. It's the seeds of sin, a harvest.

⁸The harvest you reap reveals the seed that was planted. If you plant the corrupt seeds of self-life into this natural realm, you can expect to experience a harvest of corruption. If you plant the good seeds of Spirit-life you will reap the beautiful fruits that grow from the everlasting life of the Spirit. (Galatians 6:8 TPT)

²⁰So he got up and went to his father. But while he was still a long way off, his father saw him and was filled with compassion for him; he ran to his son, threw his arms around him and kissed him. (Luke 15:20 NIV)

God doesn't punish sin. Sin punishes sin!

Jesus is now painting for us a picture of the true heart of Father God. He's a Father Who doesn't judge, condemn, shame, or put guilt on us, a Father Who knows that our life of sin has already done all that to us. God doesn't punish sin. Sin punishes sin! He's a Father Who cleanses us from all our unrighteousness, blots out our past sins, and gives us a clean slate. With open arms, He kisses us, and says, "It's party time. We need to celebrate! It's a time of laughter, fun, and joy in Kingdom living!"

¹⁰The thief does not come except to steal, and to kill, and to destroy. I have come that they may have life, and that they may have it more abundantly. (John 10:10 NKJ)

Father God is saying. "Let's restore what the canker worm has eaten in your life. It's time to rebuild, and it's time to believe for seven times' restoration what the devil has stolen." (Proverbs 6:30-31)

Father God through Christ Jesus reveals to us what being in the Kingdom of Grace is about. We aren't religious. There is no fun in religion. In God's Kingdom, it's party time, an abundant life of love, joy, favor, success, health, wealth, peace, and where we go from blessing to blessing. Wow! What you believe is what you will get.

We are in the New Covenant of Grace. We have an open door into the Kingdom of God where everything has already been lavished on us by the Father, His love gift to us. It's free! We now come into the house of God with the family where we sing and worship God, where God provides us with the best food and in all the excitement, the presence of God falls on us. We're renewed, charged, and accelerate in Him! We get high in the Holy Spirit Who edifies us and brings us into supernatural joy, love, and abundant life. This is where the blessings of God become real to us. This is where we find protection, security, and a time of fellowshipping with the family, knitted together in love.

19Consequently, you are no longer foreigners and strangers, but fellow citizens with God's people and also members of His household, 20built on the foundation of the apostles and prophets, with Christ Jesus Himself as the Chief Cornerstone. (Ephesians 2:19-20 NIV)

When I say "party," it's not what the world calls a party. The world's party is full of sins, drugs, and addictions. The party in the Kingdom of God is a true party full of the Holy Spirit and getting high on the presence of God. God created this earth for His kids to enjoy life and to have fun with our family and friends, a time of doing the things we enjoy together. God created you to have fun, and create fun with your family. Grace met the needs of fun, laughter, and enjoyment in your life as well as a fun life with your family.

Go on family vacations, family outings, have family games, watch movies together. Laugh together. Pray together and worship together. Be free to enjoy each other.

This is the life of grace. What do you enjoy? Just do it. You can trust the Holy Spirit to tell you "no" in grace if it's wrong because He said He would.

The Word says if you are going the wrong way, you will hear a voice, the voice of the Holy Spirit telling you which way to walk.

21Whether you turn to the right or to the left, your ears will hear a voice behind you, saying, "This is the way, walk in it." (Isaiah 30:21 NIV)

You can trust the Holy Spirit to tell you "no" in grace if it's wrong because He said He would.

It's the Word of God and the Holy Spirit and not religion to tell you which way to go. The Holy Spirit was sent to you. Let's get the right image of Father God and our life in the Kingdom. God will never go beyond what you expect.

What did the religious group say about Jesus because He just didn't fit into their image of God?

19The Son of Man came eating and drinking, and they say, "Look, a glutton and a winebibber, a friend of tax collectors and sinners!" (Matthew 11:19 NKJ)

We know Jesus never sinned, but to the religious groups, everything is sin. There is no abundant life, no fun, no joy, just abuse. We need to meditate on this, get the right picture in us, and get free of the wrong picture. Father God made this earth for us to enjoy and not for the world.

77

²¹And the son said to him,

"Father, I have sinned against heaven and in your sight, and am no longer worthy to be called your son."

²²But the father said to his servants,

"Bring out the best robe and put it on him, and put a ring on his hand and sandals on his feet. ²³And bring the fatted calf here and kill it, and let us eat and be merry; ²⁴for this my son was dead and is alive again; he was lost and is found."

And they began to be merry.'" (Luke 15:21-24 NKJ)

How does the father respond to the situation? Bring the best of robes, clothe my son in righteousness, for he is clean in Christ. Put the ring of authority in the Kingdom of God on my son's hand.

¹⁸Then Jesus came to them and said,

"All authority in heaven and on earth has been given to Me." (Matthew 28:18 NIV)

When we get born again, it's a time of celebration.

The father told them to put sandals on His feet.

³I will give you every place where you set your foot... (Joshua 1:3 NIV)

The enemy is under your feet. It's time to celebrate!

When we get born again, it's a time of celebration. We were dead, and now we're alive again! We were lost, but now we are found.

The oldest son, a picture of the Old Covenant, was angry because he was depending on His good works to win his father's love and blessing. He was depending on what he could do. The law under the Old Covenant was a covenant between God and us, but we can't be good enough to earn God's favor and holiness. Under the Old Covenant of the law, there is no joy, no blessings, or favor, just the heavy task master. The law condemns, shames, puts guilt on us or we just get full of pride in our own performance.

28But he was angry and would not go in. Therefore his father came out and pleaded with him. 29So he answered and said to his father,

"Lo, these many years I have been serving you; I never transgressed your commandment at any time; and yet you never gave me a young goat that I might make merry with my friends. 30But as soon as this son of yours came, who has devoured your livelihood with harlots, you killed the fatted calf for him." (Luke 15:28-30 NKJ)

The New Covenant is between God and Christ and we get to share in it because we are in Christ, connected to His good works, His performance. So, it's not dependent on us, but on Christ and what He has already done. We are full of grace in Christ, so we go from blessing to blessing.

16From the fullness of His grace we have all received one blessing after another. (John 1:16 NIV)

Who is the Father God? He's a Father Who loved me while I was yet a sinner, Who sent His Son to pay for all my past, present and future sins that became a curse for me so I could be in the family of God, a child of the Most High, loved unconditionally and all that heaven contains is now mine in Christ.

1See what great love the Father has lavished on us, that we should be called children of God! (1 John 3:1 NIV)

God doesn't remember your past failures. Father God gave me a vision, and it so helped me! When I look behind, in the past, all I see is a white board with nothing on it. If the board has nothing on it, then God doesn't see our past mistakes. They are gone! That was a life-changing moment for me. So we need to come into agreement with God. You take a moment and look back and see a white board with nothing on it. Be free of the past!

WOW! A Father Who delights in me!

³As for the saints who are on the earth,

"They are the excellent ones, in whom is all My delight." (Psalms 16:3 NKJ)

---

*Our precious Father God is
overwhelmed with joy because we are His.*

We fulfill all of God's desires. Our precious Father God is overwhelmed with joy because we are His. A Father Who is unable to contain His emotions for us. He shouts for joy when He looks at us.

¹⁷The LORD your God is in your midst, a Warrior Who saves. He will rejoice over you with joy; He will be quiet in His love [making no mention of your past sins], He will rejoice over you with shouts of joy. (Zephaniah 3:17 AMP)

³⁰Then I was beside Him as a master craftsman; and I was daily His delight, rejoicing always before Him, ³¹Rejoicing in His inhabited world, and My delight was with the sons of men. (Proverbs 8:30-31 NKJ)

I love this scripture because this is how I feel when I'm with my family. I'm totally satisfied. They are my delight and I take pleasure in being with them, and this is the very heart of God towards us. He takes pleasure in us. We are His daily delight (pleasure), and He has fun being with us. Our Father is with us, laughing in our world He has fun with us, and He loves being with us. You remember those times you are with your family laughing and laughing. Believe me, my family is so much fun! You never forget those times and they bring so much joy and satisfaction to your heart.

35Who shall separate us from the love of Christ? Shall trouble or hardship or persecution or famine or nakedness or danger or sword? 36 As it is written:

"For your sake we face death all day long; we are considered as sheep to be slaughtered."

37No, in all these things we are more than conquerors through Him Who loved us. 38For I am convinced that neither death nor life, neither angels nor demons, neither the present nor the future, nor any powers, 39neither height nor depth, nor anything else in all creation, will be able to separate us from the love of God that is in Christ Jesus our Lord. (Romans 8:35-39 NIV)

Nothing can remove God's passionate love for us that He lavishes on us. Father God pours over us His passionate love for us.

5Now hope does not disappoint, because the love of God has been poured out in our hearts by the Holy Spirit Who was given to us. (Romans 5:5 NKJ)

God overwhelms us with His love. He's a Father of too much because He sees us in Jesus. He is a loving Father Who has not withheld one thing from us in the Kingdom because of His grace.

29For those God foreknew He also predestined to be conformed to the image of His Son, that He might be the firstborn among many brothers and sisters. (Romans 8:29 NIV)

Let's practice this exercise:

> Close your eyes and imagine a loving Father
> (your Father God) looking at you.
> His eyes are filled with joy and delight.
> See Him smiling, laughing out loud.
> Now let yourself think, you are the reason for His happiness.
> He adores you, enjoys you, celebrates you, favors you and
> loves you with His complete love,
> and this never changes.
> This is grace!

As I would do this, I experienced this feeling. It felt like I was reading a fairy tale story. That was the feeling inside. Because a fairy tale is not a reality, it wasn't in my belief system of my heavenly Father towards me. I knew I had so much work to do because my image inside of Father God was religious, stern, not happy, and hard to please. Some of us never had a father, or our father had lots of problems or addictions or was very abusive or never accepted us. Whatever it is, we must change the image of our heavenly Father inside by taking what doesn't seem real and meditating on the true image of Him until it's a reality.

Prayer for Right Image of God

Lord, in the name of Jesus, I rid myself of the false image of You, the lie of the enemy, the tradition, the religion, and the legalism that's in me. I say, "No, and I renounce it and call it sin. It's got to go. It cannot live in me any longer!" I receive Who You really are, Father God, now, and I allow the image of You to become a reality in me: that You are a loving God Who delights in me and takes pleasure in me. That You celebrate me, laugh with me and love me unconditionally. That You give me favor, joy and enjoy me completely in Jesus Name. Amen

Let's look at the New Covenant of Grace that allows us to experience the love the Father has for us and to become His precious children. First of all this Covenant of Grace comes by revelation. I had head knowledge of grace for years and believed in grace, but it wasn't until I received revelation of grace that my life changed, and it became heart knowledge. I changed from religion and legalism to life and life more abundantly: a life now of too much, a life from victory to victory, a life of freedom from stress and a life where the blessings are working for me, a life of deep intimate friendship with the Father God. I'm free to love, free to give, free to forgive, and free to bless others. What a great life I have! Thank you, Jesus! He took me from the bottom of the barrel, and through grace, He brought me to the top.

I changed from religion and legalism
to life and life more abundantly...

You must realize, this revelation of grace can't be found in the intellect. It's in the supernatural. God wants you to receive the revelation of grace that's a heart knowledge from the Holy Spirit. It's in the invisible place of God.

18So we fix our eyes not on what is seen, but on what is unseen, since what is seen is temporary, but what is unseen is eternal. (2 Corinthians 4:18 NIV)

The Holy Spirit is there to show you what grace is. You can't comprehend it with the natural mind.

11I want you to know, brothers and sisters, that the gospel I preached is not of human origin. 12I did not receive it from any man, nor was I taught it; rather, I received it by revelation from Jesus Christ. (Galatians 1:11-12 NIV)

If Paul had to receive it that way, we need to receive it that way.

Well, what is the difference between Old Covenant and New Covenant? We need a full understanding of this. In the Old Covenant, Moses brought the law. (What we can do.)

17For the law was given through Moses; grace and truth came through Jesus Christ. (John 1:17 NIV)

Jesus brought grace and truth in the New Covenant (what Jesus did). The Old Covenant is obsolete because you can't have two covenants at one time. The Old Covenant is two sided, bilateral. It's between God and man. The Old Covenant is conditional because man is in the mix. The Old Covenant was what man wanted to do, so God made blood covenant with man through the blood of an animal because a covenant needs blood. The covenant was conditional, so it was based on blessing and cursing. If you did everything under the law, then you are blessed. If you missed it, then you are under a curse.

10For all who rely on the works of the law are under a curse, as it is written: "Cursed is everyone who does not continue to do everything written in the Book of the Law." (Galatians 3:10 NIV)

Well, we couldn't do it, but God gave us the Old Covenant, the law to show us we couldn't do it, that we needed a Redeemer. The Old Covenant is conditional, based on our behavior. It's two sided between man and God and it's temporal because we failed.

The New Covenant is not dependent on us. It's dependent on Christ now so it can't fail.

Now the New Covenant of Grace is unconditional because it is unilateral (one sided). We are not in the mix. Christ Jesus went into the Holy of Holies with His blood, and sprinkled it on the mercy seat seven times (which is the number of completion). The Old Covenant is completed and now no more. The mercy seat becomes the throne of grace and a New Covenant was created with the blood of Christ Jesus between Father God and Jesus; we are in Christ and His works. The New Covenant is not dependent on us. It's dependent on Christ now so it can't fail. It's eternal It's supernatural, and we are connected to the works of Christ. So the New Covenant is now only blessing and blessing if we are leaning on the works of Christ. Because of Christ, we are now heirs of God, joint-heirs of Christ, and children of God. The New Covenant can't fail because Jesus didn't fail.

Where we can miss it is when we take the Old Covenant, which is obsolete, with our performance of doing and doing by our good works, and try to mix with what Christ has already done. It doesn't work!

[17]*Neither do people pour new wine into old wineskins. If they do, the skins will burst; the wine will run out and the*

wineskins will be ruined. No, they pour new wine into new wineskins, and both are preserved. " (Matthew 9:17 NIV)

[17]*This means that the covenant between God and Abraham was fulfilled in Messiah and cannot be altered. Yet the written law was not even given to Moses until 430 years later, after God had "signed" His contract with Abraham! The law, then, doesn't supersede the promise since the royal proclamation was given before the law.* (Galatians 3:17 TPT)

This verse explains that the Messiah, Christ Jesus, fulfilled the covenant between God and Abraham, and it cannot be altered.

[8]*And the Scripture, foreseeing that God would justify the Gentiles by faith, preached the Gospel to Abraham beforehand, saying, "In you all the nations shall be blessed."* (Galatians 3:8 NKJ)

Let's look at what happened here. God is the Alpha and Omega. He began and He finished and then He began. God wishes that none would perish. God planned everyone to be saved, but because of freedom of choice, not everyone will be saved.

[4]*...Who desires all men to be saved and to come to the knowledge of the truth.* (1 Timothy 2:4 NKJ)

God already knew Adam and Eve would blow it and before the foundation of the world, God saw Jesus crucified.

[8]*...the Lamb Who was slain from the foundation of the world.* (Revelation 13:8 NKJ)

So the Gospel of Grace was already in the finished work of God. God preached the Gospel to Abraham by taking him into the unseen, and He showed Abraham the death, burial, and resurrection of Christ Jesus.

⁸And the Scripture foreseeing that God would justify the Gentiles by faith preached the Gospel to Abraham beforehand... (Galatians 3:8 NKJ)

Abraham believed God, and *it was accounted unto him for righteousness* because he believed in the Gospel of Grace.

³Abraham believed God, and it was accounted unto him for righteousness. (Romans 4:3 NKJ)

The Old Testament is a picture of the inward working of the New Covenant. Abraham was a picture of the life of grace. When I come into the New Covenant of Grace, I entered into all the blessings of Abraham.

⁹And so the blessing of Abraham's faith is now our blessing too! (Galatians 3:9 TPT)

The Covenant of Grace is blessing and blessing.

²⁰Now, a mediator does not represent just one party alone, but God fulfilled it all by Himself! (Galatians 3:20 TPT)

God Himself spoke directly to Abraham, and God fulfilled it all by Himself. Abraham was a picture of believing in the works of Christ. He was in the life of blessings. Wherever Abraham went, he got favor and blessings.

You can't fail in Christ Jesus.
You've been set up to always win!

The New Covenant of Grace is believing that God has already finished your destiny in the unseen, and it's up to you to receive it and let it flow from your life into others. You can't fail in Christ Jesus. You have been set up to always win! Grace doesn't make you lazy, but grace fuels your passion, grace energizes.

⁹My passion is to enlighten every person to this divine mystery. (Ephesians 3:9 TPT)

Grace causes you to work harder than them all, yet not you but the grace of God.

¹⁰...I worked harder than them all – yet not I, but the grace of God that was with me. (1 Corinthians 15:10 NIV)

Grace is freedom, it's power, it's passion, it's energy. Grace is the very works of Christ Jesus in you wanting to be revealed through your every-day life.

⁴So, my brothers and sisters, you also died to the law through the body of Christ, that you might belong to another, to Him Who was raised from the dead, in order that we might bear fruit for God. (Romans 7:4 NIV)

The Word of God tells us that we are to die to the law and live in the New Covenant of Grace, but we have a freedom of choice.

³³ "This is the covenant I will make with the people of Israel after that time,"

declares the LORD.

"I will put My law in their minds and write it on their hearts. I will be their God, and they will be my people." (Jeremiah 31:33 NIV)

In the New Covenant God is saying, "I will, I will, I will," and He did, He did, He did! But the Old Covenant is, "If you, if you, if you." In the New Covenant, we are not in the equation. It's all about what God will do, and our part is to believe and receive.

Let's clarify the picture here. Old Covenant – blessing and cursing. New Covenant – blessing and blessing. Old Covenant is bilateral: God and man in the mix with animal blood. It's temporal because we couldn't keep it. The New Covenant is unilateral, one sided (we aren't in the mix) because it's between God and Jesus with the blood of Christ Jesus. The New Covenant is eternal. It's the life of the supernatural naturally.

From Blessing to Blessing
Chapter 7

How many of us have gotten back under the law, the Old Covenant, after being saved? This is what Paul is dealing with here. The Old Covenant is gone and we are now under a New Covenant, a Covenant of Grace, what Christ has done, His works. The New Covenant of Grace couldn't happen until the curse of the Old Covenant was fully paid and Jesus fulfilled the law. The Old Covenant is done. Now it's time to make a paradigm shift from the Old Covenant, what we do, to the New Covenant, what Christ has done.

Make a paradigm shift from the Old Covenant, what we do, to New Covenant, what Christ has done.

---

⁶I marvel that you are turning away so soon from Him Who called you in the grace of Christ, to a different gospel, ⁷which is not another; but there are some who trouble you and want to pervert the Gospel of Christ. (Galatians 1:6-7 NKJ)
⁷That is a fake "gospel" that is simply not true. There is only one Gospel – the Gospel of the Messiah! Yet you have allowed those who mingle law with grace to confuse you with lies. (Galatians 1:7 TPT)

Calling the Old Covenant the gospel is a lie. There is only one Gospel and it's the Gospel of Jesus, the Messiah. When we mingle the law with grace, we get confused with lies.

What this is saying is, trying to add in your good works with what Christ has done, mixing them together, doesn't work.

5So too, at the present time there is a remnant chosen by grace. 6And if by grace, then it cannot be based on works; if it were, grace would no longer be grace. (Romans 11:5-6 NIV)

If it's work, then it's not grace. Jesus did a complete work. My responsibility is to believe, surrender to it, and receive it, and then let His works flow through me. The Word of God says that if you get under the law, what you do, grace can't get to you. You step out of the covering of who you are in Christ.

What are the blessings that are yours in the New Covenant? The most powerful words that God first spoke into us is He blessed us.

22God blessed them... (Genesis 1:22 NIV)

The last words that Jesus spoke over us is He blessed us.

51While He was blessing them, He left them and was taken up into heaven. (Luke 24:51 NIV)

51While He was still speaking out words of love and blessing, He floated off the ground into the sky, ascending into heaven before their very eyes! (Luke 24:51 TPT)

1Now it shall come to pass, if you diligently obey the voice of the LORD your God, to observe carefully all His commandments which I command you today, that the LORD your God will set you high above all nations of the earth. 2And all these blessings shall come upon you and overtake you, because you obey the voice of the LORD your God. (Deuteronomy 28:1-2 NKJ)

Under the Old Covenant, it's "*if* you fully obey," you will be blessed. Under the New Covenant, the word *if* isn't in the equation because Jesus fully obeyed, and we are in Him.

¹If you fully obey the Lord your God and carefully follow all His commands I give you today, the Lord your God will set you high above all the nations on earth.

²All these blessings will come on you and accompany you if you obey the Lord your God:

³You will be blessed in the city and blessed in the country.

⁴The fruit of your womb will be blessed, and the crops of your land and the young of your livestock—the calves of your herds and the lambs of your flocks.

⁵Your basket and your kneading trough will be blessed.

⁶You will be blessed when you come in and blessed when you go out.

⁷The Lord will grant that the enemies who rise up against you will be defeated before you. They will come at you from one direction but flee from you in seven.

⁸The Lord will send a blessing on your barns and on everything you put your hand to. The Lord your God will bless you in the land He is giving you.

⁹The Lord will establish you as His holy people, as He promised you on oath, if you keep the commands of the Lord your God and walk in obedience to Him.

¹⁰Then all the peoples on earth will see that you are called by the name of the Lord, and they will fear you.

¹¹The Lord will grant you abundant prosperity—in the fruit of your womb, the young of your livestock and the crops of your ground—in the land he swore to your ancestors to give you.

¹²The Lord will open the heavens, the storehouse of His bounty, to send rain on your land in season and to bless all the work of your hands. You will lend to many nations but will borrow from none.

^{13}*The Lord will make you the head, not the tail. If you pay attention to the commands of the Lord your God that I give you this day and carefully follow them, you will always be at the top, never at the bottom.* (Deuteronomy 28:1-13 NIV)

Connect to what He has already done. In Him I go from blessing to blessing. In the Old Covenant, <u>God will</u> but in the New Covenant <u>God did.</u>

This is so exciting to believe, receive and let it flow through you so that the blessings overtake you. One translation says the blessings will chase you down, be too much so that you are blessed, your children and grandchildren are blessed, whatever your hands touch is blessed, and all your possessions are blessed!

The blessings will chase you down, be too much!

Deuteronomy 6:10-12 says there is land with your name on it.

^{10}*When the LORD your God brings you into the land He swore to your fathers, to Abraham, Isaac and Jacob, to give you – a land with large, flourishing cities you did not build,* ^{11}*houses filled with all kinds of good things you did not provide, wells you did not dig, and vineyards and olive groves you did not plant – then when you eat and are satisfied,* ^{12}*be careful that you do not forget the LORD, Who brought you out of Egypt, out of the land of slavery.* (NIV)

There are houses that are already yours filled with all the goodies and businesses that are already yours in your destiny. There are also ministries with your name on them that you are to sow into. Your name is already on all of this. Now receive them as done.

⁷The LORD will grant that the enemies who rise up against you will be defeated before you. They will come at you from one direction but flee from you in seven. (Deuteronomy 28:7 NIV)

Testimony

The enemy is a bully, and he plays on our inner vows we have made in the past. Years ago as we stood on the blessing, God blessed us with a beautiful home that was way beyond us. We knew our name was on it because we always ask God before we buy if our name is on the house. So stepping in faith because we were filled with the anointing when we walked into this gorgeous home, we knew it was God's will for us. Our name was on it, except that once we were living in it, I was filled with guilt and embarrassment for living in such a beautiful home. I couldn't enjoy it.

As I went to the Holy Spirit to find out what the trouble was, the Holy Spirit revealed to me an inner vow I had made, "I would never be materialistic." So, I felt I was violating my inner treaty and was ashamed.

Let's look at this. It was God's will for us to have this home, but I can't enjoy the blessing so the blessing became my enemy.

I broke the inner vow in Jesus' name because this home was a gift from Father God! God has streets of gold and large pearly gates. I was totally set free to enjoy Father God's gift to me.

¹⁹Moreover, when God gives any man wealth and possessions, and enables him to enjoy them, to accept his lot and be happy at his work – this is a gift of God. (Ecclesiastes 5:19 NIV84)

God's heart for His children is to enjoy life and have life and life more abundantly. It's so important that we make the paradigm shift in our minds that the blessing will fight for you.

⁸But even if we, or an angel from heaven, preach any other gospel to you than what we have preached to you, let him be accursed. (Galatians 1:8 NKJ)

What this scripture is saying is when you get back under the law, you are under a curse. Well, what does that mean? The word *curse* there means you are devoted for destruction.

¹⁰But if you choose to live in bondage under the legalistic rule of religion, you live under the law's curse. For it is clearly written: "Utterly cursed is everyone who fails to practice every detail and requirement that is written in this law! (Galatians 3:10 TPT)

It's a free choice. We choose. We need to die to the law to live under the Covenant of Grace so the blessings that are already ours have a voice in our lives. We are then free to live in health, wealth, favor, going from blessing to blessing, living a Kingdom life. Let the blessings fight for you.

Testimony

It was years ago when I heard that health was ours.

²⁴...by Whose stripes you were healed. (1 Peter 2:24 NKJ)

With that information, I did have that moment of saying to myself, "You mean I can never be sick again?" I thought,

"No one will be able to feel sorry for me again. I don't know if I want to give that up."

What was happening? I had a covenant with sickness. I used to pretend to be sick just to stay home from school. Sickness was my comforter, and now I had to give it up, and let the Holy Spirit be my Comforter.

I had a covenant with sickness.

The blessing wants to fight for you. The blessing will reveal to you where you made that covenant, treaty or inner vow against the blessing so the Holy Spirit can set you free to live in the fullness of the blessing.

I received the blessing of health over forty years ago. I took authority over my body and spoke the blessings over it. I blessed my body, its organs, blood and all the cells.

Don't wait until sickness hits you. Speak to your body every day, and use your words.

8The harvest you reap reveals the seed that was planted. If you plant the corrupt seeds of self - life into this natural realm, you can expect to experience a harvest of corruption. If you plant the good seeds of Spirit-life you will reap the beautiful fruits that grow from the everlasting life of the Spirit. (Galatians 6:8 TPT)

What is this scripture saying? If you plant the seed of sin consciousness, if you plant the seed of focusing on self and not keeping your eyes on Jesus, not fixing your heart on the promises, what you already have in the unseen...

3Fix your heart on the promises of God and you will be secure, feasting on His faithfulness. (Psalm 37:3 TPT)

...if you don't focus on the promises, what will you have? Well, in the natural realm, you can expect a harvest of corruption. Did you get that?

If I give myself to sin consciousness, and if I am focusing on self, I am planting seeds of corruption. I put myself back under the law, what I can do, and I am planting seeds of corruption. Then we blame God and say,

"God is teaching me something."

No! It's not being responsible for your own decisions in life. What are you choosing? Are you choosing the law or grace?

Now grace doesn't make you lazy. Grace energizes you, it's full of passion and it activates you to fulfill destiny. It's not you, but grace working through you. (Ephesians 3:9, 20 TPT)

[18]The law, then, doesn't supersede the promise since the royal proclamation was given before the law. If that were the case, it would have nullified what God said to Abraham. We receive all the promises because of the Promised One—not because we keep the law! (Galatians 3:18 TPT)

Paul received the Gospel of Grace by revelation. The word *revelation* in the following scripture means the unveiling of the otherwise unknown, to enlighten. Grace can't be found or understood with head knowledge but only by the supernatural of the Holy Spirit. It's what is in the unseen being made seen.

[11]I want you to know, brothers and sisters, that the Gospel I preached is not of human origin. [12]I did not receive it from any man, nor was I taught it; rather I received it by revelation from Jesus Christ. (Galatians 1:11-12 NIV)

What Paul is saying by the inspiration of the Holy Spirit is that the New Covenant is the revealing of grace by the revelation of the Holy Spirit. It's not found by human origin. Paul was frustrated with the Galatians because they had left the life of grace and were under the law. Paul, by the inspiration of the Holy Spirit, fully understood the problem. They had received the Gospel of Grace in the intellect and not by revelation.

Testimony

In my own life, I came into the saving knowledge of Christ, got born-again and over the years, sat under people who taught on grace. I read their books, and saw things I needed to change that were religious and legalistic, but on the whole I didn't have a revelation of grace. In prayer one day, I'm sure I was led by the Holy Spirit, I asked about my destiny. I had some very serious questions for God. His answer to me was that I was *"called of God to preach the message of grace for such a time as this"* and then the Holy Spirit overpowered me with His presence, and the revelation of grace hit me.

It changed my life at that moment! Then began the paradigm shift in my own life. I went from my own good works to His good works, from me trying to earn in my own human effort to already having it. In prayer, I would be trying to create my tomorrow by my confession of His Word instead of knowing it was already done in the unseen. My prayer was now in agreement to take what's already done in the unseen and bring it into the seen. I went from never reaching my expectation with lots of hard work, to going beyond my expectation with my total dependence on Him. Through this paradigm shift, I know God's promises don't fail, I know He is good, and I know the supernatural God of miracles. Most importantly, I was getting free from self-works to living in Christ's works.

⁴Through these He has given us His very great and precious promises, so that through them you may participate in the divine nature, having escaped the corruption in the world caused by evil desires. (2 Peter 1:4 NIV)

I was coming into a total rest that I already have it, and that He had set me up to win, and more than win, in every situation. I've truly stepped into life and life more abundant on every side. I love the grace life! My heart is to build His Kingdom and to see such power and victory, with such ease, is a dream come true!

²⁰Never doubt God's mighty power to work in you and accomplish all this. He will achieve infinitely more that your greatest request, your most unbelievable dream, and exceed your wildest imagination! He will outdo them all, for His miraculous power constantly energizes you. (Ephesians 3:20 TPT)

I'm living this verse now.

They were not fully realizing that they can't, but Jesus did!

In his letter to the Galatian church, Paul was realizing that they didn't have a revelation of grace, that in their hearts was a bunch of rules and "do's" by human effort. They were not fully realizing that they can't, but Jesus did, that the Old Covenant is obsolete and of the natural, but the New Covenant is of the supernatural.

²⁴These two women and their sons express an allegory and become symbols of two covenants. (Galatians 4:24 TPT)

Because the New Covenant is of the supernatural, it has to come by revelation, the life of grace. I believe Paul realized the problem. He had painted a beautiful picture of the crucifixion, but they received it as head knowledge and not heart revelation. Paul began to pray that they would come into revelation of the Gospel of Grace.

[17]*I keep asking that the God of our Lord Jesus Christ, the glorious Father, may give you the Spirit of wisdom and revelation, so that you may know Him better.* (Ephesians 1:17 NIV)

Paul writes in the letter to the Ephesians that they were to pass this letter on to all the churches. Paul was making this his prayer, and he continued praying revelation on them. He realized they needed to have a supernatural revelation from God to live and understand the life of grace in the New Covenant.

Revelation brings us into truly knowing our Father God and Who He really is. It brings us into an intimate relationship with our loving Father because we know it's what Christ has done that gives us this amazing relationship with our Father God. Revelation opens our eyes into the unseen realm where God lives, knowing that grace energizes us. Grace doesn't make us lazy, but we work harder than them all in grace, but it's not work. It's passion, it's excitement, it's a joy and it's pleasure! Grace propels us into our destiny with God's power. It makes destiny easy and fun and the best life ever. In the fullness of grace, we go from one blessing to another.

[9]*My passion is to enlighten every person to this divine mystery.* (Ephesians 3:9 TPT)

[8]*Grace alone empowers me…* (Ephesians 3:8 TPT)

[16]*From the fullness of His grace we have all received one blessing after another.* (John 1:16 NIV84)

⁸God's plan all along was to bring this message of salvation to the nations through the revelation of faith. (Galatians 3:8 TPT)

It's not your faith. It's now His faith you connect your faith to.

²...looking unto Jesus, the author and finisher of our faith... (Hebrews 12:2 NKJ)

¹⁶...above all, taking the shield of faith with which you will be able to quench all the fiery darts of the wicked one. (Ephesians 6:16 NKJ)

⁵Let me ask you again: What does the lavish supply of the Holy Spirit in your life, and the miracles of God's tremendous power, have to do with you keeping religious laws? The Holy Spirit is poured out upon us through the revelation and power of faith, not by keeping the law! (Galatians 3:5 TPT)

²...through Whom we have gained access by faith into this grace in which we now stand. (Romans 5:2 NIV)

The Blessings are Working for You
Chapter 8

The Old Covenant is of the natural, and it's what you do. The New Covenant is of the supernatural, and it's what Christ has already done.

²³Ishmael, the son of the slave girl, was a child of the natural realm. But Isaac, the son of the freewoman, was born supernaturally by the Spirit – a child of the promise of God! ²⁴These two women and their sons express an allegory and become a symbol of two covenants. (Galatians 4:23-24 TPT)

The Old Covenant makes you sin-conscious because you are looking at what you see in the natural, but the New Covenant makes you Christ-conscious. You're looking at what He has done in the unseen. When I have my eyes on Christ Jesus, I see blessing and blessing because Jesus is full of grace. So, in Him, I'm full of grace. When I look at Jesus, I come into agreement with what He has already done, and the blessings are released to work for me.

We see that the law puts us under slavery because we don't have the power to get free of the addictions and things we don't want to do. What we look at, we become! The child by the natural realm (picture of Old Covenant) is unable to see by the Spirit. The son of the free woman (picture of New Covenant) sets you free to see by the Spirit to be able to live in the supernatural realm. Seeing into the unseen, we see the finished works of Christ, and then we are able to believe, agree, and receive.

Now, in the New Covenant, I am able to bind myself to the promises of God, and call them mine in Christ Jesus. I am able to fasten myself to the promises of God because the supernatural is working in my life to produce the promises for me. The New Covenant moves on my behalf and produces that miracle.

When we are in the Covenant of Grace, the scriptures open us up to the unseen and produce revelation in us for that scripture. It will open us up to the revelation of faith in grace.

Jesus is our beginner of faith.

²Let us fix our eyes on Jesus, the author and perfecter of our faith... (Hebrews 12:2 NIV84)

For years I have said this scripture, but I never saw Jesus as the author of my faith. I thought I was the author.

Author means "starter" of our faith. We are not it! Jesus starts it. When we think we are the author, the beginner, we are doing our own thing again. We become an earner and not a receiver. We get in that awful cycle of work, work, work! I have to have enough faith. We get under the law and into fear.

Jesus' faith will take you into realms
that you can never take yourself.

We are in grace. Receive Christ Jesus, your starter of faith, and let grace empower you into the Christ faith that moves mountains and brings forth miracles in your every-day life.

You will never have enough faith because Jesus is the starter of your faith. So, bind yourself to His faith. Jesus is the Word of God and faith comes by hearing the Word of God. (Romans 10:17) Become one with it, bind yourself to it. Jesus' faith will take you into realms that you can never take yourself. Jesus' faith is pure and will drive out the unbelief in your heart.

God wants us to realize that we need to be totally dependent on the Word of God, Jesus. Think of a baby in the womb of the mother. The baby is totally dependent on the mother for its food, oxygen, and blood. That's us in the life of Christ. We are dependent on the works of Christ being the receiver like the baby in the womb. The baby isn't an earner in the womb but a receiver. It's already done! Now believe, receive, and let it flow to bless others.

When I step into the faith of Christ, it opens the door for me to step into the life of grace.

²*...through Whom we have gained access by faith into this grace in which we now stand.* (Romans 5:2 NIV)

Now faith works by love.

⁶*...but faith working through love.* (Galatians 5:6 NKJ)

⁶*All that matters now is living in the faith that is activated and brought to perfection by love.* (Galatians 5:6 TPT)

Activated by love, faith is energized to go to work. My love won't make it, but the love of God in my heart that is unconditional, will activate faith and get it working to produce. When I step into God's love, bind myself to it, surrender to God's love, I step into God's realm because God is love.

⁴*...God is love.* (1 John 4:8 NIV)

I know, in and of myself, I can't love the way God's Word says I should love. The love of God puts faith into action to bring forth what is in the unseen, in the Kingdom of God. This is what God gave us to set us up to be winners!

Now, in the love of God, Who He is, I step into being a partaker of His divine nature and into the fruit of the Holy Spirit working in my life. It releases the miraculous of faith to work on my behalf to produce the miracles and blessings. It takes me from poverty to wealth, from sickness to health. It takes me from rejection to supernatural favor, from self-centeredness to Jesus-centered.

What happens here? I take on the thoughts of Christ, (mind of Christ) connecting to the thoughts of Christ. His thoughts are that I go from blessing to blessing, from life to abundant life, from love to love, from favor to favor, from wealth to wealth, from health to health, to build and produce in God's Kingdom. Seeing signs and wonders in every area, not only in my life, but in the lives of others.

8Heal the sick, cleanse the lepers, raise the dead, cast out demons. Freely you have received, freely give. (Matthew 10:8 NKJ)

2I will make you into a great nation, and I will bless you; I will make your name great, and you will be a blessing. (Genesis 12:2 NIV)

My mouth is full of miracles because His Word is in my mouth.

Blessed to be a blessing and knowing that God, every day, has fulfilled my destiny, and I connect to that. Seeing it as He sees it. Not only do I take on His thoughts, I take on His words. Praise God! The Bible says grace gives me good words.

6Let every word you speak be drenched with grace... (Colossians 4:6 NIV)

I can't tame my tongue, but guess what? Christ tamed it. So, now I take on the sword of the Spirit which is the Word of God in my mouth. My mouth is full of miracles because His Word is in my mouth. What I say is what I will produce, and it produces the action of faith.

Take time to think about this. I know in my own life I've done this. We claim certain weaknesses about our children, and we actually hold them in it because of our authority over them. Our words keep them in bondage to it. Set them free today by changing your confession. Our words frame their lives.

³*By faith we understand that the worlds were framed by the Word of God, so that the things which are seen were not made of things which are visible.* (Hebrews 11:3 NKJ)

If we don't like the way their life looks, then we better reframe it. We need to say what God says.

Let's move on. The Word says that Christ was full of grace and truth. So we are full of grace and truth.

¹⁴*We have seen His glory, the glory of the One and only Son, Who came from the Father, full of grace and truth.* (John 1:14 NIV)

In grace we go from blessing to blessing. I'm full of grace because I'm surrendered to Christ, to all that He is, and as He is, <Christ> so am I in this earth. These are the words we need to say.

¹⁰*But if you choose to live in bondage under the legalistic rule of religion, you live under the law's curse. For it is clearly written: "Utterly cursed is everyone who fails to practice every detail and requirement that is written in this law!"* (Galatians 3:10 TPT)

If you choose to live in legalistic bondage, you are responsible for your choice.

Testimony

When I was dedicated to the legalistic rule of religion, I went from curse to curse. I would take one step forward and two steps back. This was my life for the first five years of being born-again. Then the Holy Spirit set me free from that life. Praise God! Sometimes, it takes your children to say something that the Holy Spirit can use to open your eyes to the truth. One of my sons said to me,

"I'm not going to serve God because I see what you go through."

Under the law, we were under a curse, always sick, living in poverty, depressed, and on and on. Now my sons serve God today. Those words of my son set us free from legalistic bondage of the Old Covenant. They made us stop and say,

"The fruit is not good."

Then when we surrendered it to God, the Holy Spirit was able to open our eyes, and it was the beginning of our freedom. The faith of a child!

10But if you choose to live in bondage under the legalistic rule of religion, you live under the law's curse. For it is clearly written: "Utterly cursed is everyone who fails to practice every detail and requirement that is written in this law!" (Galatians 3:10 TPT)

Testimony

In my own life I was so committed to the law. When you are under law, you are in control because you must be sure you are keeping it, and you are the boss. Guess what! You become your own Holy Spirit, and now everything is wrong and you are fear driven. And before long, you become addicted to the law, and you come to the end of the law one day, and you can't go on with it. You cry out for help.

The Holy Spirit began to walk me out from living under the law, to letting go of the control and allowing the Holy Spirit to retrain me to be Spirit led. The Holy Spirit said to me,

"You are sin conscious; you are addicted to the law."

By letting go of the control and giving control to the Holy Spirit, He could then tell me if I did something wrong. And when I fell into my old ways, the Holy Spirit would say,

"Did I tell you that you did something wrong?"

"Well, no."

"Then it's not wrong."

I learned to trust the Holy Spirit to do His job in my life. I'm totally free today to trust the Holy Spirit and to keep my eyes on Jesus.

[13] *Yet, Christ paid the full price to set us free from the curse of the law. He absorbed it completely as He became a curse in our place. For it is written: "Everyone who is hung upon a tree is doubly cursed."* [14] *Jesus, our Messiah, was cursed in our place and in so doing, dissolved the curse from our lives, so that all the blessings of Abraham can be poured out upon even non-Jewish believers. And now God gives us the*

promise of the wonderful Holy Spirit who lives within us when we believe in him. (Galatians 3:13-14 TPT)

God is looking for a people who will embrace what Christ, His Son, has already done. We are free from the heavy yoke of the law to now live in what Christ has done, which never fails.

God is looking for a people who will embrace what Christ, His Son, has already done.

This is how the system is set up. You have freedom of choice, to choose the law or grace, to choose faith in what Christ has already done and fasten yourself to the promises of God: faith or law, life or death, blessings or curses. You have the freedom to choose, but God says, "Choose life and blessings."

[19]This day...I have set before you life and death, blessings and curses. Now choose life, so that you and your children may live. (Deuteronomy 30:19 NIV)

The law demands complete obedience in all things. You must do all of the law without any compromise. You are either a law keeper or a law breaker. It's an absolute standard. Even one little error can mar your record. It's like a small spot of jam on your wedding dress. It spoils the whole dress. One nail flattens the tire. So one broken commandment spoils you and then comes the flood of the curse – not good.

Let's choose Christ. Let's let Him be your Author. Let Him be your Beginner, let Him be your All in all.

[28]Come to Me, all you who are weary and burdened, and I will give you rest. (Matthew 11:28 NIV)

Let go, and let Jesus be in charge. He did it all! It's done so you can live an amazing, abundant life with all the blessings. Let grace have the voice in your life and be your teacher and mentor.

Earlier in this chapter we talked about the New Covenant, a covenant of the supernatural and that the Old Covenant is of the natural. It has no power to set you free or change your life or break strongholds off your life. The Old Covenant is about what you do. In the New Covenant I don't live by what I see, I live by the Word of God, I live by what I don't see, the unseen, the invisible, the very Word of God. In the New Covenant God makes a way where there is no way.

23Ishmael, the son of the slave girl, was a child of the natural realm. But Isaac, the son of the freewoman, was born supernaturally by the Spirit – a child of the promise of God! 24These two women and their sons express an allegory and become symbols of two covenants. The first covenant was born on Mt Sinai, birthing children into slavery –children born to Hagar. (Galatians 4:23-24 TPT)

The son of the free woman was of the supernatural, the New Covenant, free from bondages, free from addictions, free from sickness, free from poverty, and on and on – freedom! Freedom from depression, destruction, worthlessness, and rejection.

Testimony

My oldest son, and his wife, came over after they missed their ultrasound. They were a half-hour late. He began to tell me about their basement being flooded. They had four children at the time, and one of their sons woke them up to tell them that they had a swimming pool in their basement, so all their furniture was ruined. Also, they had just installed new wood floors upstairs, but it all had to be pulled up and re-installed which would mean all their furniture would have to be put in the garage for however long it would take to re-install the floors. He continued on telling us about his life at this time. He had asked a friend of his to put a TV in the back seat for the children to watch movies. Well, when he got his car back, the seats in the back were ruined and the TV didn't work.

After hearing all of this, I said to him,

"I'm so sorry you are having such a bad day."

He immediately corrected me by saying,

"I only have blessed days! My life is totally blessed in every way. God is good."

Now that wasn't just a great confession. He believes that! Nine years later my son is beyond blessed. He lives by the Word of God, the unseen, and fastens himself to the promises of God and keeps his eyes on Jesus. He believes the New Covenant of the supernatural, the promises are yes and amen in Christ. He is the example of how to live successfully in the New Covenant. He doesn't allow the enemy to give him a bad day because the enemy is defeated. He is under our feet. As my son told me,

"I don't give the enemy any attention, and Jesus says the blessings are mine and they work for me. And you know, in the New Covenant, God always makes a way where there is no way."

In the New Covenant, we keep our eyes on Jesus, the Word, fastened to the promises and believe the blessings are working for us, that the blessings are ours. We believe that God does miracles in the midst of a disaster, a failure. God turns all things into good.

In the New Covenant of Grace we must realize that we need the righteousness of Jesus because we can't be good enough to be righteous or earn our own righteousness.

21I do not set aside the grace of God, for if righteousness could be gained through the law, Christ died for nothing! (Galatians 2:21 NIV)

So Christ, through His death, burial, and resurrection, earned and gave us His righteousness.

30What then shall we say? That the Gentiles, who did not pursue righteousness, have obtained it, a righteousness that is by faith; 31but the people of Israel, who pursued the law as the way of righteousness, have not attained their goal. 32Why not? Because they pursued it not by faith but as if it were by works. They stumbled over the stumbling stone. (Romans 9:30-32 NIV)

Testimony

This was my major battle - letting go of my own righteousness. I grew up in a home where we didn't go to church much. I was that person in high school working to be the best at school, an over-achiever, exhibiting a behavior that was upright, like the teacher's pet.

I worked hard at being good. I had so many rules that I gave myself, and I kept them all! If anything, being righteous was my biggest success in life, I thought. When I realized I had to give up my own righteousness and take on His, "Oh my gosh!" My head said, "This is right and true and you need this." But my heart said, "No way!" It was a battle. It probably was my biggest battle. I tried and tried to get rid of the pride of self-righteousness. Finally, I had to admit it was an addiction, like some people have an addiction to drugs or alcohol. At that point, I was free to embrace His righteousness.

³And since they've ignored the righteousness God gives, wanting instead to be acceptable to God because of their own works, they've refused to submit to God's faith-righteousness. (Romans 10:3 NIV)

I didn't know the righteousness of God as a teenager, and I sought to establish my own.

See, I didn't know the righteousness of God as a teenager, and I sought to establish my own. So I couldn't submit to God's righteousness.

³And since they've ignored the righteousness God gives, wanting instead to be acceptable to God because of their own works, they've refused to submit to God's faith-righteousness. (Romans 10:3 NIV)

⁶But we are all like an unclean thing, and all our righteousnesses are like filthy rags. (Isaiah 64:6 NKJ)

I wanted God to be proud of me, I wanted to hold up my good works to God to say, "Look what I have done!"

We see this very situation in the Apostle Paul's life in the third chapter of Philippians. Paul is telling us about his own struggles with self-righteousness and what he did to get free.

⁸What is more, I consider everything a loss because of the surpassing worth of knowing Christ Jesus my Lord, for whose sake I have lost all things. I consider them garbage, that I may gain Christ ⁹and be found in Him, not having a righteousness of my own that comes from the Law, but that which is through faith in Christ—the righteousness that comes from God on the basis of faith. (Philippians 3:8-9 NIV)

You must give up your own self-righteousness to get to know Christ. Now I was saved. People can be saved and still set aside His righteousness to hold on to their own self-righteousness to live by their own good work. For the sake of Christ Jesus, we lose all of our own self-righteousness, for they are like filthy rags to God. The Apostle Paul considered them garbage.

People can be saved and still set aside His righteousness.

The reward of giving up our own self-righteousness is gaining Christ and to know Him and be found in Him. We can strive to be perfect by diligently keeping the law in our own righteousness, but we will fail. And if we think we are righteous in what we do, we are deceived. Our righteousness to God is like filthy rags.

6But we are all like an unclean thing, and all our righteousnesses are like filthy rags... (Isaiah 64:6 NKJ)

No one has ever been declared righteous by the works of the law. God said even before Christ died that the righteous will live by faith.

4...but the righteous shall live by his faith. (Habbakuk 2:4 NIV84)

It's not Christ plus my works. Christ or the law, blessings or the curse, faith or your works; you choose.

There was no curse for Abraham but only blessings. Why? Because Abraham believed God. And we in the New Covenant, under the Abrahamic blessings, believe God.

³What does Scripture say? "Abraham believed God, and it was credited to him as righteousness." (Romans 4:3 NIV)

⁵And this hope is not disappointing fantasy, because we can now experience the endless love of God cascading into our hearts through the Holy Spirit Who lives in us. (Romans 5:5 TPT)

Abraham believed God. Well what did he believe?

⁸And the Scripture, foreseeing that God would justify the Gentiles by faith, preached the gospel to Abraham beforehand, saying, "In you all the nations shall be blessed." (Galatians 3:8 NKJ)

Abraham believed the New Covenant in the unseen, and it made Him righteous. God took Abraham into the future and preached the Gospel to Him. Wow!! Abraham lived the grace life. By his believing, he took what was in the future and brought it into the now and lived in the blessings of the works of Christ.

¹The Lord had said to Abram, "Go from your country, your people and your father's household to the land I will show you. ²"I will make you into a great nation, and I will bless you; I will make your name great, and you will be a blessing ³I will bless those who bless you, and whoever curses you I will curse; and all peoples on earth will be blessed through you .(Genesis 12:1-3 NIV)

Now through the death, burial, and resurrection, the Gospel of Grace, God did make you into a great nation. God did bless you. God did make your name great. You are a blessing, etc.

That's how faith looks! Call what's not as though it is. In the New Covenant there is no curse. You go from blessing to blessing. The blessings are working for you.

A Blood Covenant that Can't Fail
Chapter 9

The Blood Covenant was between God and Christ for us.

¹⁷This means that the Covenant between God and Abraham was fulfilled in Messiah and cannot be altered. (Galatians 3:17 TPT)

The Covenant cannot be altered or changed because the Messiah fulfilled it. Now Abraham saw it fulfilled in the future, but there was a day that the Messiah actually came and walked this earth. He was 100% man and 100% God, and He fulfilled the Gospel of Grace that we live in now.

We don't always understand Abraham's life, but one thing Abraham understood was that he was imperfect and needed a Messiah. He believed God, and because He believed God, it was credited to him as righteousness, and he received the Covenant of Grace, the works of Christ Jesus.

²⁰ Now, a mediator does not represent just one party alone, but God fulfilled it all by Himself! (Galatians 3:20 TPT)

Get the picture in the Old Testament that God didn't need Abraham to fulfill the covenant. God did it all by Himself.

¹³For when God made a promise to Abraham, because He could swear by no one greater, He swore by Himself. (Hebrews 6:13 NKJ)

God is saying, "I had to make this covenant all by Myself because I don't lie so when I make a promise it can't fail."

¹⁴saying, "Surely blessing I will bless you, and multiplying I will multiply you." (Hebrews 6:14 NKJ)

"I will bless you, Abraham, I will!" And He did and He

did and He did! And God multiplies the blessings in our lives and keeps on multiplying them.

So the Covenant of Grace, the New Covenant is not based on how good I am, but how good Jesus was and how Jesus is in my life. It's all on Jesus. I just fasten myself to Jesus, the Word, and believe God; now I'm a receiver. This changed my life. If you get this revelation, it will change your life.

I just fasten myself to Jesus, the Word,
and believe God; now I'm a receiver.

This is the Old-Testament picture of the Abrahamic Covenant that God painted. God is giving Abraham the Covenant promise, and Abraham is asking, "How will I know?"

8But Abram said,

"Sovereign LORD, how can I know that I will gain possession of it?"

9So the LORD said to him,

"Bring me a heifer, a goat and a ram, each three years old, along with a dove and a young pigeon."

10Abram brought all these to Him, cut them in two and arranged the halves opposite each other; the birds, however, he did not cut in half. (Genesis 15:8-10 NIV)

In the Old Testament we see pictures of the New Covenant of Grace for us under the Covenant of Abraham. Looking at the life of Abraham, God appears to him to make blood covenant with Abram. Abram gets so excited that God is telling him what to do. Abram follows all God's orders, and

117

when Abram is ready to make blood covenant with God, God puts him to sleep.

12As the sun was setting, Abram fell into a deep sleep... (Genesis 15:12 NIV)

Jesus, the Word, walks on the blood between the animals. Jesus, here is a picture of the smoking fire pot with a blazing torch.

17When the sun had set and darkness had fallen, a smoking firepot with a blazing torch appeared and passed between the pieces. 18On that day the LORD made a covenant with Abram... (Genesis 15:17-18 NIV)

2But who can endure the day of His coming? Who can stand when He appears? For He will be like a refiner's fire or a launderer's soap. 3He will sit as a refiner and purifier of silver; He will purify the Levites and refine them like gold and silver. Then the Lord will have men who will bring offerings in righteousness. (Malachi 3:2-3 NIV)

11I baptize you with water for repentance. But after me comes One Who is more powerful than I, Whose sandals I am not worthy to carry. He will baptize you with the Holy Spirit and fire. (Matthew 3:11 NIV)

29"Is not my Word like fire," declares the LORD, "and like a hammer that breaks a rock in pieces? (Jeremiah 23:29 NIV)

27See, the Name of the Lord comes from afar, with burning anger and dense clouds of smoke; His lips are full of wrath, and His tongue is a consuming fire. (Isaiah 30:27 NIV)

God was showing us that we couldn't keep the Covenant, that we are imperfect beings. Jesus brings us the Covenant of Grace, the Blood Covenant. This Covenant would have to be made between God and Jesus, the perfect One.

^{20} *Now, a mediator does not represent just one party alone, but God fulfilled it all by Himself!* (Galatians 3:20 TPT)

Jesus, the Word, is the New Covenant of Grace. He is the fire that burns up the plans of the devil in our lives. This is an illustration of what God showed me. If I was living in Los Angeles, there is a thick smog in the morning over the city, but the sun burns it off. It's like that in our lives. We wake up in the morning, and the enemy has plans to ruin our day, but Jesus, the Word, is a fire that burns up the plans of the enemy over us. He is that consuming fire.

Jesus, the Word, is the fire that burns up the plans of the devil in our lives.

God has plans for you. Jesus already gave you life and life more abundantly for each day so that Jesus' favor and victory could go forth, and that you go from blessing to blessing, the Covenant of Grace working for you!

Understanding that the Abrahamic Covenant is a picture of the Covenant of Grace changed my life. Somehow I thought I was a part of the covenant. Believing that, put me under the curse, living from condemnation to condemnation, from guilt to guilt, being sin conscious.

You must see that you can't keep the Blood Covenant and that it's between God and Jesus so it can't fail. I thought I could. I was deceived. We are imperfect beings, and if you break one part of the covenant, you broke it all. I thought I could earn the blessings. Once I totally understood that I'm not a part of the Blood Covenant, but it totally depends on God and Jesus, I am now a receiver of the Blood Covenant blessings. This was one of those life-changing moments for me.

13For when God made a promise to Abraham, because He could swear by no one greater, He swore by Himself, 14saying, "Surely blessing I will bless you, and multiplying I will multiply you." (Hebrews 6:13-14 NKJ)

God is not a man that He should lie. The promise can't fail in the Covenant of Grace. God has already blessed us and is multiplying the blessing to us.

Our mouths are a creative force in our lives that frame our day. Speak out those blessings! Burn off the chaff of the day, and step into the blessings for that day!

God visited Moses through a burning bush and told him to go and set His people free from slavery.

10 So now, go. I am sending you to Pharaoh to bring my people the Israelites out of Egypt. (Exodus 3:10 NIV)

Moses, through nine plagues, couldn't set them free. But when Moses applied the blood of the lamb to the door post, the blood totally set God's people free from bondage. They left Egypt with all the wealth of the world, and there was none sick among them.

37He brought them forth also with silver and gold: and there was not one feeble person among their tribes. (Psalm 105:37 KJV)

This was a picture of the New Covenant Blood of Jesus. The perfect blood that can't fail. There is power in the blood as they headed for the land flowing with milk and honey, the Promised Land.

Now the people wanted to make covenant with God. They wanted the covenant between them and God. We would have our part of keeping the law, and God would have His part. Under the law, we had to obey the whole law. If we broke one, we broke them all, and we would be under the curse. (Deuteronomy 28:15-68 NIV)

We can't fully obey. We are imperfect beings! Why was the law given? It was given to show us we need a Savior, Christ Jesus.

22But the Scriptures make it clear that since we were all under the power of sin, we needed Jesus! And He is the Savior Who brings the promise to those who believe. (Galatians 3:22 TPT)

We can't fully obey. We are imperfect beings!

In Christ Jesus we are free from the law, we are free from religion, and we are free from the curse. The law makes you an earner and grace makes you a receiver. We needed Jesus because we were under the power of sin.

56The sting of death is sin, and the power of sin is the law. (1 Corinthians 15:56 NIV)

The power or strength of sin is the law. So when I put myself under the law, I find out I can't do it. It's like this,

23...the law was a jailor, holding us as prisoners under lock and key... (Galatians 3:23 TPT)

The law, what we do, is our jailor. We may have an addiction, let's say alcohol, and we decide to stop drinking. We get rid of all the booze in the house, but by noon we are at the liquor store buying booze. Then we can't stop drinking until it's all gone. Whatever the addiction or generational curse is, it controls us. We don't control it. It must have its pleasure.

Another example is, I say, "I'm going to walk in love," until something happens that's not loving, then into jail I go.

It's the same with making the decision to choose favor or joy or wealth or health. I can't do it in my own strength! Jesus already did it! Love, favor, joy, wealth, health and on and on, it's all mine in the works of Christ. He gave it all.

In college they teach if you are in a certain class of people, you will never get out, and it will go down to your children and to your grandchildren and on and on. Why? Because we don't have the power in and of ourselves. If we do go up another level, we will destroy that level subconsciously because it's above our image inside. We can't take the stress; it's uncomfortable.

His gift of love and favor now cascades over us...

Grace gives us the power to be free from addictions and from a poor self-image. Grace sets us free to love, to live in all the blessings, to have them multiplied in our lives and feel comfortable with them. Through grace, we know that we belong with all of the blessings because Christ made us comfortable and at rest in them.

[24]...God freely gives away His righteousness. His gift of love and favor now cascades over us, all because Jesus, the Anointed One, has liberated us from the guilt, punishment, and power of sin! (Romans 3:24 TPT)

[24]The law becomes a gateway to lead us to the Messiah so that we would be saved by faith. (Galatians 3:24 TPT)

[25]But when faith comes the law is no longer in force, since we have already entered into life. (Galatians 3:25 TPT)

[29]And since you've been united to Jesus the Messiah, you are now Abraham's "child" and inherit all the promises of the Kingdom-realm! (Galatians 3:29 TPT)

The Blood Covenant, made between God and Jesus, put us into the family of God as His precious children.

⁶And so that we would know for sure that we are His true children, God released the Spirit of Sonship into our hearts – moving us to cry out intimately, "My Father! You're our true Father!" (Galatians 4:6 TPT)

We see that God wants us to know that we are His children. He released the *Spirit of Sonship into our hearts* so that we would be moved to intimately confess God as our true Father.

Maybe we didn't have a father, or not a good father, but God has provided the Spirit of Sonship to be more than enough, an over-the-top Father for us. God sets us free from the lack. We need to believe this promise, embrace it and declare this, "God is my true Father!" Then let Him supernaturally fill the void.

I know, in myself, that I didn't have a father per se, but when I got born again, I never felt the lack of a father because I felt close to Father God. Looking back, I know I believed the Spirit of Sonship that was deposited in my heart. We need to meditate on this promise until it becomes a reality in us.

³³Their faith fastened onto their promises and pulled them into reality. (Hebrews 11:33 TPT)

This promise needs to become a reality to us to set us free from a wrong image of a father or the lack of a father. We need to trust in the Spirit of Sonship to form the true image of the Father in us, and out of that, we will experience the relationship of a perfect father, the Father God.

²I will make you into a great nation, and I will bless you; I will make your name great, and you will be a blessing. (Genesis 12:2 NIV)

He already made us a great nation because we are in the family of God. God goes on to say He will bless us. Well, He has already blessed us because we are in the Abrahamic Covenant.

I will make your name great. He will make my name great. I thought, "This is interesting." As I would confess this promise for years, I would think, "I don't need my name great, oh well." The Holy Spirit said to me one day, "It's not your name. It's His name that you are wearing now because you are His child." Oh, okay now I understand.

It is very important to understand that we have His name just like my two sons in our family. They bear our name, they wear our name, and our name is now their name. What does that mean to us?

It's His name you are wearing now because you are His child.

God's name, ELOHIM, Creative Power; God has given me the ability to create my tomorrow by what I think, visualize and say.

His name, EL SHADDAI, is all the blessings are mine, the blessings are working for me. *Have no doubt, I promise to bless you over and over...and multiply you without measure.* (Hebrews 6:14 TPT) I go from blessing to increase of blessing each and every day.

ADONAI, I have been given all authority to take dominion over every situation in my life, to bring it into obedience to the Word of God.

JEHOVAH TSIDKENU is now my Righteousness. I wear His righteousness.

JEHOVAH M'KADDESH, holiness, not my holiness. It's His holiness I wear that gives me the ability and power to be free from addictions in His holiness. I take on the divine nature of God, and escape the corruption of this world caused by evil desires. (2 Peter 1:4)

JEHOVAH JIREH, He provides. God has already provided everything in the Kingdom of God for me, and the Kingdom of God lives in me.

JEHOVAH NISSI, He covers me in victory in my defeated areas, those places where I missed the mark. God, my restorer, turns those things into victory! Praise God!! I'm more than a conqueror. I have victory wherever I go. He restores what the canker worm has eaten. God is my Redeemer.

He's my JEHOVAH SHALOM. I wear His peace now, but not only that, shalom also means prosperity. I'm clothed in prosperity. Wealth and riches are in my house. (Psalm 112:3) Jesus became poor that I could now live in His riches. (2 Corinthians 8:9)

He's my JEHOVAH SHAMMAH. He abides with me. He covers me with Himself.

He is my JEHOVAH ROPHE. He has already clothed me in health. I have healing power. The dead will be raised, the blind will see, the deaf will hear, freely I receive, freely I give wherever I go.

He is my JEHOVAH ROHI. He is my Shepherd I shall not want. (Psalm 23)

All of these names are now ours in Christ Jesus and they identify us.

[14] *For this reason I kneel before the Father,* [15]*from whom every family in heaven and on earth derives its name.* (Ephesians 3:14-15 NIV)

Paul is telling us that we wear the Father's name now. This is very humbling to know, and it should cause us to kneel before Him in honor.

³*Every spiritual blessing in the heavenly realm has already been lavished upon us as a love gift from our wonderful heavenly Father, the Father of our Lord Jesus—all because He sees us wrapped into Christ. This is why we celebrate Him with all our hearts!* (Ephesians 1:3 TPT)

I'm not earning Father God's love.
I'm loved now because I exist.

Our hearts need to be filled with thanksgiving and honor to our Father God. We are an heir of God, His precious children, made joint-heirs with Christ Jesus, the Head. We are His body, made one with the Word of God. This is great news!

⁷*Now we're no longer living like slaves under the law, but we enjoy being God's very own sons and daughters! And because we're His, we can access everything our Father has – for we are heirs of God through Jesus, the Messiah!* (Galatians 4:7 TPT)

We are not under the law. I'm not earning Father God's love. I'm dead to the law. I'm under grace, the works of Christ Jesus. I'm loved now because I exist. We now enjoy being Father God's own sons and daughters, and because we are His, we can access everything that is His because we are one with Christ Jesus.

I think of my own sons. They have access to everything we have. If they need it, we provide it and always more than they need. So everything of ours is theirs, and they know that. We, as parents, love this part of parenthood, but we do want them to be thankful and appreciative. I expect them to rise up and call me blessed and praise me. (Proverbs 31:28) We expect them to honor us. (Ephesians 6:2)

This is our part, not only to believe and receive and let it flow from us to others, but to be thankful and appreciative to honor our heavenly Father. Do we know that we have access to everything of the Father God? Do we know that?

We know everything that the Father God has is ours. Now what is our relationship with the Father God? Well, we are dearly loved.

¹Follow God's example, therefore, as dearly loved children ²and walk in the way of love, just as Christ loved us and gave Himself up for us as a fragrant offering and sacrifice to God. (Ephesians 5:1-2 NIV)

God wants us to know that we are loved, and He wants us to experience that love. As Christ walked in that love, we are to walk in that same love. In the Kingdom life, it's not about us. It's about others.

I was thinking about my husband. He was the most amazing father my sons could ever have in the natural. I would be overcome with so much joy by the way he would lay down his life for our sons. I could not have asked for a better father for them, but my husband had an amazing father also. And now I watch my sons being loving, serving fathers to their children, following in the footsteps of their father. As we submit to the Spirit of Sonship, we will follow in the footsteps of our Father God.

¹See what great love the Father has lavished on us, that we should be called children of God! And that is what we are! The reason the world does not know us is that it did not know Him. (1 John 3:1 NIV)

Father God so desires us to experience His love for us. It's important to know that we are loved and cherished by Father God, and to allow the Holy Spirit to reveal this in our lives. God's Word says that Father God is a Father to the fatherless. (Psalm 68:5) He is no respecter of persons. (Acts 10:34) So in His Kingdom, you don't lack.

With Father God, there might be a time we need a little more extra attention than usual.

I can remember there was a time that we felt that our younger son needed a little extra time with his father. We set everything up so that could happen in the family. Well, with the Father God, there might be a time we need a little extra attention than usual. We might be dealing with abandonment or insecurity or in a storm in our life, and Father God is right there to meet our need and more. We must believe and receive that from Him. The Word of God tells us,

[16]*The Spirit Himself testifies with our spirit that we are God's children.* (Romans 8:16 NIV)

Oh my gosh! It's the Holy Spirit that makes Father God real to us. The Holy Spirit is whispering in our innermost being. He talks to us, telling us that we are God's beloved child, loved by the Father God. You must take that moment to believe that, receive it, and meditate on it so it can become a reality in your life. All the promises become a reality to me by my believing, receiving and letting it flow out of me to touch others.

Now, the love of God is not based on our religious duties.

[15]And you did not receive the "spirit of religious duty," leading you back into fear of never being good enough. But you have received the "Spirit of Full Acceptance," enfolding you into the family of God. And you will never feel orphaned, for as He rises up within us, our spirits join Him in saying the words of tender affection, "Beloved Father!" (Romans 8:15 TPT)

God is not demanding perfection from you. He is not demanding that you earn His love. You are not under fear of not being good enough.

[7]For God has not given us a spirit of fear, but of power and of love and of a sound mind. (2 Timothy 1:7 NKJ)

You have been given, by the Father God, the Spirit of full acceptance because you exist. Now God wants us to declare to Him with tender affection, "Beloved Father!" Just like we like to hear, as parents, words of tender affection of our children's love for us, the Father God just melts when we say those words to Him. Knowing this from within, that it's not about what you do, but that He loves you just the way you are, unconditionally.

[9]But now that we truly know Him and understand how deeply we're loved by Him, why would we, even for a moment, consider turning back to those weak and feeble principles of religion, as though we were still subject to them? (Galatians 4:9 TPT)

[10]Why would we want to go backwards into the bondage of religion —scrupulously observing rituals like special days, celebrations of the new moon annual festivals, and sacred years? (Galatians 4:10 TPT)

God is saying, "Stop it! You are free from all that." Begin meditating on truly getting to know your Father God and understanding how deeply He loves you, getting to know your freedom and receiving the free love gifts He has already lavished on you because you exist and are His beloved child. Receiving the power of grace that He gives you that energizes you, fuels your passion, sets you up to win.

12 Beloved ones, I plead with you, follow my example and become free from the bondage of religion. I once became as one of you, a Gentile, when I lived among you–now become free like me. When I first came to minister to you, you did me no wrong. I can't believe you would do wrong to me now! (Galatians 4:12 TPT)

Now it's a pleading with you to say, "No" to the religious-ness of the Old Covenant. Let's look at the contrast between law and grace.

The Law takes. Grace gives.
The Law says, "Do." Grace says, "Done."
The Law says, "Work to be holy."
Grace says, "You are Holy."
The Law condemns. Grace redeems.
The Law kills. Grace gives life.
The Law brings the curse. Grace brings the blessings.
The Law reveals sin. Grace forgives sin.
The Law was written on tablets of stone.
Grace is written on the tablet of our hearts.
The Law brought bondage. Grace brought freedom.

Law is what you do.
Grace is what Christ has done.

Grace Brings Us into a Life of Love
Chapter 10

²²For it is written that Abraham had two sons, one by the slave woman and the other by the free woman. (Galatians 4:22 NIV)

Abraham had two sons, one by the free woman and one by the slave woman, which is a picture of two covenants, as I mentioned in Chapter 8. The son of the slave woman is a picture of the Old Covenant and what it's saying to us is that the Old Covenant is the outward between man and God. Because it's of the outward, of the natural, it causes us to be a slave to the prisons in our life, i.e. prisons of generational curses, addictions, sins of the flesh. The Old Covenant has no power to set you free from poverty, sickness, behaviors, addictions, etc.

The Old Covenant has no power to set you free from poverty, sickness, behaviors, addictions, etc.

The second covenant is the New Covenant, the Covenant of Grace, a covenant about the inward, a covenant that brings you into the born-again experience that sets you free from the old man. In this covenant, you become a new person, a child of God. It's a covenant of the supernatural. This is a covenant of power and ability that has totally set you free from poverty, sickness, behavior patterns of selfishness and addictions and generational curses that are passed down from one generation to the next.

Paul is trying to show us here that the Old Covenant, the Law, is obsolete, dead, gone, and no more. It didn't work. The

Old Covenant had no power, but God gave us a New Covenant of Grace through the works of Christ Jesus. We are now in the New Covenant joined to Christ, and we are in Him, where all the promises are yes and amen. (2 Corinthians 1:20) The resurrection power of the New Covenant has set us in heavenly places in Christ Jesus to be totally free from the prison of slavery of the past, present, and future.

23 Ishmael, the son of the slave girl, was a child of the natural realm. But Isaac, the son of the freewoman, was born supernaturally by the Spirit–a child of the promise of God! (Galatians 4:23 TPT)

Ishmael, the son of the slave girl, is a picture of the Old Covenant, a covenant of the natural realm with no power in it, the Law. We have all experienced the powerlessness of the Old Covenant, the Law. The Word of God says in 1 Corinthians 15:56 that the power of sin is the law.

56 The sting of death is sin, and the power of sin is the law. (1 Corinthians 15:56 NIV)

I know this too well. When I was a teenager I had a weight problem. I would decide to go on a diet in hopes of losing the weight. I would get on a plan and get all excited about the weight loss that I would experience. Now, it worked for a while, but as soon as stress came into my life, I would pig out until I overate. I would be good for about three or four days on the diet, but by the fourth day, I would be feeling deprived, and I would eat again until I could eat no more. I ate everything full of sugar and fat, and not good fat, either!

Think about people who have a drug addiction, and under the law, they get rehabilitated. Then something bad happens in their life, and they go back to the drugs because their bodies were deprived of the drugs. They can't stop. They are driven until they overdose. The power of sin is the law. The natural realm, the law, has no power to change us.

Now the son of the freewoman, a picture of the Covenant of Grace, the new Covenant, is of the supernatural. Why? Because Isaac was a child of promise. Isaac was a picture of Christ Jesus, born by the Word of God, by the Spirit, the covenant of promise. In the new Covenant of Grace we live a life of the supernatural, a covenant that has freed us from poverty, sickness, addictions, and every horrible or bad thing that could happen.

Testimony

We were out with a couple, and they were giving us their testimony of when they came to the church. They didn't know Jesus as their Savior, but as time went on, they became Christians. The husband became very ill with a 105-degree fever day after day. When he went to the doctor, they of course ran blood tests and found that he had rheumatoid arthritis which is an incurable, crippling disease. In the meantime, his wife signed them up to become members of the church, which is Living Word Bible Church in Mesa, Arizona. When that happened, he was instantaneously healed. The Word of God says those who are planted in the house of the Lord shall flourish.

[13] *...planted in the house of the LORD, they will flourish...* (Psalm 92:13 NIV)

And that the gates of hell shall not prevail against the church, (Matthew 16:18 KJV) the power of the new Covenant of Grace.

Testimony

My husband had bleeding ulcers, and he had just accepted Christ Jesus as his Lord and Savior. On the way to the doctor to set up surgery, he prayed to God to receive his healing, and was instantaneously healed at that moment. The new Covenant of Grace is all powerful, it's supernatural.

[24]These two women and their sons express an allegory and become symbols of two covenants. The first covenant was born on Mt. Sinai, birthing children into slavery–children born to Hagar. (Galatians 4:24 TPT)

In the Old Covenant under the law, you were born into slavery, into the prisons of your environment, into your family heritage, into your bad decisions, with no power to escape.

[26]In contrast, there is a heavenly Jerusalem above us, which is our true "mother." She is the freewoman, birthing children into freedom! (Galatians 4:26 TPT)

This is Isaac, a child of promise, a promise that brings freedom from our prisons of our environment, of our family, our negative heritage, and freedom from our bad decisions. This is a picture of the new Covenant of Grace: a supernatural covenant, a covenant of promise that represents the rest in God, knowing that God through Christ Jesus has already set us free, a covenant that leads us to the blessings that are working for us, a Covenant of Grace that through Christ Jesus we have life and life more abundantly!

Now Paul is painting a picture for us of two covenants expressing an allegory from Genesis 21:8-10.

[8]The child grew and was weaned, and on the day Isaac was weaned Abraham had a great feast. [9]But Sarah saw the

son whom Hagar the Egyptian had borne to Abraham was mocking, ¹⁰*and she said to Abraham, "Get rid of that slave woman and her son, for that woman's son will never share in the inheritance with my son Isaac."* (Genesis 21:8-10 NIV)

This is saying to us that you can't mix the law, what you do, with grace, what Jesus has done. You can't mix a little bit of you in what Christ has done. Why? Because it's by grace, it's not of you, so you can't boast. This comes to us by the Holy Spirit that the law will never share in the inheritance that grace gives us.

You can't mix a little bit of you in what Christ has done.

---

²⁸*Dear friends; just like Isaac, we're now the true children who inherit the Kingdom promises.* (Galatians 4:28 TPT)

²⁹*At that time the son born according to the flesh persecuted the son born by the power of the Spirit. It is the same now.* ³⁰*But what does Scripture say? "Get rid of the slave woman and her son, for the slave woman's son will never share in the inheritance with the free woman's son."* (Galatians 4:29-30 NIV)

The law will persecute us because we can't keep it. The law brings persecution, condemnation, guilt, and shame.

³¹*It's now so obvious! We're not the children of the slave woman; we're the supernatural sons of the freewoman—sons of grace!* (Galatians 4:31 TPT)

Paul, by the inspiration of the Holy Spirit, brings this up again in the Old Covenant versus the New Covenant.

³*...clearly you are an epistle of Christ, ministered by us, written not with ink but by the Spirit of the living God, not on*

tablets of stone but on tablets of flesh, that is, of the heart.
⁶Who also made us sufficient as ministers of the New
Covenant, not of the letter but of the Spirit; for the letter kills,
but the Spirit gives life. (2 Corinthians 3:3, 6 NKJ)

The Old Covenant was written on stone, not a part of you. But the New Covenant is written on our hearts by the Spirit of God. The New Covenant of Grace is in you. The Godhead lives in us, all that God is and has lives in us. It's a part of us now.

⁶...who also made us sufficient as ministers of the New
Covenant, not of the letter but of the Spirit; for the letter kills,
but the Spirit gives life. ⁷But if the ministry of death... (2 Corinthians 3:6-7 NKJ)

The Old Covenant is a ministry of death. When we are under the law, we keep losing, we fail, and we feel overwhelmed with condemnation, shame, and guilt.

⁹For if the ministry of condemnation had glory... (2 Corinthians 3:9 NKJ)

¹⁶Nevertheless when one turns to the Lord, the veil is
taken away. ¹⁷Now the Lord is the Spirit; and where the Spirit
of the Lord is, there is liberty. (2 Corinthians 3:16-17 NKJ)

The new Covenant of Grace gives you freedom from addictions, poverty, sickness, rejection, bad behavior, self, etc. because the Spirit of God lives in you. As we step into this New Covenant of Grace, we step into the works of Christ and rest in His works by the instrument of His promises. His life now flows through us.

Paul, in the fifth chapter of Galatians, is revealing to us, by the power of the Holy Spirit, the truth of the new Covenant of Grace: that through the works of Christ, we have been set free of self. In the New Covenant, we enter into a covenant of the supernatural. Every day is a day of miracles and blessings. It's a day of blessing others, for we are free from self.

¹Let me be clear, the Anointed One has set us free—not partially, but completely and wonderfully free! We must always cherish this truth and stubbornly refuse to go back into the bondage of our past. (Galatians 5:1 TPT)

...we must stubbornly refuse to go back into the bondage of our past.

---

¹³Freedom means that we become so completely free of self-indulgence that we become servants of one another, expressing love in all we do. (Galatians 5:13 TPT)

This is a revelation that our freedom is to be free of self, to be able to walk in love.

⁴You who are trying to be justified by the law have been alienated from Christ; you have fallen away from grace. (Galatians 5:4 NIV)

The Holy Spirit through Paul is saying,

"Don't get back under your good works. Stay in your freedom that Christ has provided. This is the only way to fulfill your heart's desire to love."

When we get into our performance, we alienate or sever ourselves from Christ, and the works of Christ can't work through us. We are on our own in our life with Christ. When we stand fast in our freedom in Christ, we are receivers of what Christ has already given us, what the law could never give us under the Old Covenant.

The example the Holy Spirit gave me: In a house electricity is flowing, but if the wires are severed, the electricity can't flow through the house to light up the house, or bring heat, air conditioning, etc. It's impossible. That's what happens when we get into our performance and leave the performance of Christ; the blessings can't get to us. It's impossible.

¹⁸The law, then, doesn't supersede the promise since the royal proclamation was given before the law. If that were the case, it would have nullified what God said to Abraham. We receive all the promises because of the Promised One—not because we keep the law! (Galatians 3:18 TPT)

Another translation says we fall away from the revelation of grace. See, the revelation of grace allows us to see into the unseen. It's not in the mind, the intellect. It's of the Spirit. It's in my heart.

³⁷Not one promise of God is empty of power, for nothing is impossible with God. (Luke 1:37 TPT)

This new Covenant of Grace has the power to free us from self and bring us into the love of God for others.

⁶For in Christ Jesus neither circumcision nor uncircumcision avails anything, but faith working through love. (Galatians 5:6 NKJ)

Faith is activated by God's love, and faith has the power to produce the promises that become seen in the natural.

⁶All that matters now is living in the faith that is activated and brought to perfection by love. (Galatians 5:6 TPT)

Now this freedom to love brings us into mountain-moving faith, pure faith, the very faith of Christ Jesus that carries us to victory. It's the faith that conquered kingdoms.

³³Through faith's power they conquered kingdoms and established true justice. (Hebrews 11:33 TPT)

It's faith that is brought to perfection by love, faith that fastens onto the promises of God to pull them into reality.

^{33}*Their faith fastened onto their promises and pulled them into reality!* (Hebrews 11:33 TPT)

Grace brings us into a life of love. In grace, everything in the Kingdom is already mine. In grace, I realize that my love can't work. It's conditional. I need His love that's unconditional. His love has already been written on my heart and mind. In grace, I've been made a partaker of His divine nature. In grace, I can connect to it all.

This life of love puts me into the realms of signs and wonders. It's a life of changing the natural realm and producing miracles in my every-day challenges. Praise God! Grace teaches us to live on the top in His love.

Testimony

Tom and I were saved in 1972. We started out in grace, but it wasn't long before we were under the law, or our performance. We brought the law into our marriage. Our home became full of judgement, condemnation and criticism. We loved each other, but our love wasn't working. As we entered into our tenth year of marriage, we faced the facts that things were getting worse and worse, so we went to the Holy Spirit for help. The Holy Spirit (through praying in the Spirit a half hour every night until we saw Jesus in the middle of our marriage) let us know that our marriage was under the law.

We said new marriage vows over each other that were grace vows. We broke the Old Covenant of the Law, the curse, and died to the law and bound ourselves to Christ, being now married to the new Covenant of Grace.

What was once a home full of discontentment and failure, now in the love walk, became a home full of the love of God. A cloud of love, so thick you could cut it with a knife, could be felt in our home from then on. What was impossible under the law, became way beyond what we could imagine or hope for under grace. Grace took over. We couldn't, but grace did!

What was impossible under the law, became way beyond what we could imagine or hope for under grace.

---

⁴Therefore, my brethren, you also have become dead to the law through the body of Christ, that you may be married to another—to Him Who was raised from the dead, that we should bear fruit to God. (Romans 7:4 NKJ)

Grace is a teacher, a mentor. All of a sudden, I was changing my thoughts to the good, and he was changing his thoughts. Grace gives you the power and ability. (Titus 2:11-12) I realized my love couldn't do it, and he realized his love couldn't do it. We needed God's unconditional love to rule in our marriage.

We are now living in the love of God. We are now living in the blessings of God, going from blessing to blessing, from favor to favor. We are now going into 50 years of marriage, and we are over-the-top in love with each other, best of friends. Every wonderful thing we could ever hope for, we have received in the finished work of Christ Jesus. The law couldn't do it. We wanted to do what only grace could give us. We tried and tried under the law but failed terribly because the law doesn't work. We couldn't do it. We needed a Savior, Jesus, and He already did it!

We had to understand that being under the Old Covenant of the Law was very destructive in our marriage.

Satan is a legalist who wants to get you under the law to put the curse on you. You have no power or ability to change yourself, your thought life, or your words under the law. You are on your own, but grace sets us free (of self) to love.

We need to be generous with God's love in the way our spouse or people receive love. There are five different ways we can give love. One way is a total focus on the person who is communicating with you, being an active part of the conversation. Another way is serving them. This is doing projects for them or with them. Gifts are another way we can give love. It's giving a gift that says more than the words, "I love you," a visual aid. Another way to give love is physically through hugs, touches or just being with them. And last, are words of encouragement or words that build up. Grace gives us encouraging words.

[16]*May our Lord Jesus Christ Himself and God our Father, Who loved us and by His grace gave us eternal encouragement and good hope,* [17]*encourage your hearts and strengthen you in every good deed and word.* (2 Thessalonians 2:16-17 NIV)

That's what grace gave Dr. Tom and I, a love that was an action, a love that gave.

[34]*A new command I give you: Love one another. As I have loved you, so you must love one another.* (John 13:34 NIV)

[14]*For Christ's love compels us, because we are convinced that one died for all, and therefore all died.* (2 Corinthians 5:14 NIV)

The love of Christ will move me, urge me, pressure me, push me, and drive me forcibly! The love of Christ is an action that helps the needy, cares for others, gives finances, prays for the sick and moves in signs and wonders. God has wrapped us up in His love, because God is love. (1 John 4:8)

[10]God is not unjust; He will not forget your work and the love you have shown Him as you have helped His people and continue to help them. (Hebrew 6:10 NIV)

The love of Christ will move me, urge me,
pressure me, push me and drive me forcibly!

What I want you to see is, first of all, faith works by God's love that brings us into the life of grace.

[6]All that matters now is living in the faith that is activated and brought to perfection by love. (Galatians 5:6 TPT)

This is where you see mountain-moving faith, pure faith, faith that conquers kingdoms!

[37]Not one promise from God is empty of power, for nothing is impossible with God! (Luke 1:37 TPT)

When you're under the works of Christ, covered in the love of Christ, clothed in the love of God, God is able to do impossibilities because He already did it through Christ.

[13]Beloved ones, God has called us to live a life of freedom in the Holy Spirit. But don't view this wonderful freedom as an opportunity to set up a base of operations in the natural realm. Freedom means that we become so completely free of self-indulgence that we become servants of one another, expressing love in all we do. (Galatians 5:13 TPT)

This scripture tells us how love looks in grace. Freedom means we are totally free from self-indulgence. We are free now by the Holy Spirit to serve one another in love. Love is an action. You decide to love. Love is doing. When you are under the law, you are very sin conscious. We become what we are looking at. Under the law, we become very self-centered. We are then living in a very self-centered world of condemnation, guilt and judgement, and it's all about me.

The life of grace brings us into the love of God, and set's us free from self, addictions and the curse. In grace, we step into His divine nature and now we have the ability to step into God's love that completes the law of God, love.

[14]*For love completes the laws of God. All of the law can be summarized in one grand statement: "Demonstrate love to your neighbor, even as you care for and love yourself."* (Galatians 5:14 TPT)

Grace-A Life of the Holy Spirit
Chapter 11

Grace gives us powerful words that create. Grace gives us God words that are loving words. God's Word says that no man can tame the tongue. So in and of myself, I can't tame my tongue. I need God to be in control of my tongue because through the death, burial and resurrection, I'm joined to Christ, and Christ is the Head that tames my tongue and gives me grace words.

15If you bite and devour each other, watch out or you will be destroyed by each other. (Galatians 5:15 NIV)

8but no human being can tame the tongue. It is a restless evil, full of deadly poison. (James 3:8 NIV)

Testimony

I remember when we first moved to Arizona in 1976, I read the book by Charles Capps, *The Tongue, A Creative Force.* I'd never heard a message on the tongue and that the power of life and death is in the tongue. Well, when I finished, I thought to myself, "I can do that!" Under the law, we think we can do it ourselves. This is our own religious thinking, "I can do that!"

I found the promises in God's Word and started confessing them. I had a plan. Now, confessing the Word of God is a good thing, but one day, by the revelation of Jesus that says no human can tame the tongue, it hit me! "I think I can, but God says I can't, and I have in and of my own strength, been trying to do it." As I finally realized what God's Word was saying, "That since I can't tame the tongue, this must be the absolute truth because God doesn't lie. So, there must be a solution! There must be something that God has provided for the tongue." I began the research to discover what I needed to do to create my tomorrows. The first thing I found was in the fourth chapter of Hebrews:

2*...they didn't join their faith with the Word. Instead, what...they heard didn't affect them deeply, for they doubted.* (Hebrews 4:2 TPT)

12*For the Word of God is living and powerful, and sharper than any two-edged sword, piercing even to the division of soul and spirit, and of joints and marrow, and is a discerner of the thoughts and intents of the heart.* (Hebrews 4:12 NKJ)

12*For the Word of God is living and active and full of power [making it operative, energizing, and effective].* (Hebrews 4:12 AMP)

Wow!!

17*Take the helmet of salvation and the sword of the Spirit, which is the Word of God.* (Ephesians 6:17 NIV)

The sword of the Spirit isn't in my hand!
It's in my mouth! It's His tongue!

We know that the sword of the Spirit is part of the armor of God. Now, I had this image that the sword was in my hand. The sword of the Spirit is the Word of God. As I'm praying, and realizing that no man can tame the tongue, "Oh my goodness! The sword of the Spirit isn't in my hand! It's in my mouth! It's His tongue!"

16*...and coming out of His mouth was a sharp, double-edged sword.* (Revelation 1:16 NIV)

[15]Coming out of His mouth is a sharp sword with which to strike down the nations. (Revelations 19:15 NIV)

I realized, at that moment, that God has tamed our tongue by giving us His tongue, the sword of the Spirit, the awesome power that grace provides. We can't, but grace did!

In the Covenant of Grace, we have revelation that we can't, but grace has done it. Grace is knowing the sword of the Spirit is in your mouth, and that you can't do it, but Christ has already done it. You are fastened to the Word of God, and it's Christ in you speaking God's Word through you.

[13]And we articulate these realities with the words imparted to us by the Spirit... (1 Corinthians 2:13 TPT)

I've had to say to myself, "I can't tame the tongue, so I put on the tongue of Christ Jesus, the sword of the Spirit, in my mouth to speak God's Word, the words imparted to me by the Spirit."

[15]Coming out of His mouth is a sharp sword with which to strike down the nations. (Revelations 19:15 NIV)

Oh my goodness! Let's put this all together. When you step into and connect to God's love, the love that activates faith, and you have the tongue of Christ Jesus, that is the sword of the Spirit, you are stepping into mountain-moving faith!

[22]Jesus replied, "Let the faith of God be in you! [23]Listen to the truth I speak to you: If someone says to this mountain with great faith and having no doubt: 'Mountain, be lifted up and thrown into the midst of the sea,' and believes that what he says will happen, it will be done." (Mark 11:22-23 TPT)

Let the faith of God be in you now! This is saying we need the faith that Christ has given us. We speak to the mountain with no doubt in our heart, because we have entered into the faith that Christ Jesus has already provided. Doubt cannot live there because we have given our self to the love of

God that activates faith. With the faith of God, we enter into the tongue of Christ Jesus, the sword of the Spirit, and we have whatever we say, believing and receiving it is done already.

Now I want you to move the sword of the Spirit out of your hand into your mouth...

Now I want you to move the sword of the Spirit out of your hand, into your mouth, seeing it come out of your mouth. This is the vision I want you to meditate on this week. This is how you get the revelation moving in your own heart. It's the power of life in the tongue submitted to God.

In my own life, I was talking to my husband one day, "Honey, I really thought I could tame the tongue until this scripture jumped out at me, ...*no man can tame the tongue.*" (James 3:8 NIV84) What a revelation! My husband said, "I can tell you, you can't tame your tongue." Well, honesty does prove the Bible. How we deceive ourselves by thinking we can, when God's Word says we can't.

Jesus said this in Matthew 17.

[20]*Truly I tell you, if you have faith as small as a mustard seed, you can say to this mountain, "Move from here to there," and it will move. Nothing will be impossible for you."* (Matthew 17:20 NIV)

Have faith...as a mustard seed, which is the smallest of all seeds, but a mustard seed is a hybrid already. It can't be cross-bred. You can't make it better than what it is. It is a perfect seed. What Jesus is saying is that you don't have to have great faith. You need to have pure faith, the faith that Jesus has already given us.

Now Paul was saying in the fifth chapter of Galatians that faith is activated by love. So when I choose God's love, I've entered into pure faith, the faith of Christ Jesus (the Author of my faith) the mustard-seed faith. Jesus is saying with this kind of faith, nothing will be impossible for you.

⁶All that matters now is living in the faith that is activated and brought to perfection by love. (Galatians 5:6 TPT)

Let's talk about grace words.

³²Now I commit you to God and to the Word of His grace, which can build you up and give you an inheritance among all those who are sanctified. (Acts 20:32 NIV)

These grace words give you the power and ability to receive your inheritance that you already have. I see it like this, grace words activate what you already have in you and bring it into reality to be seen and function. The grace words make what's invisible visible in your life. Grace words are words that are powerful, that build up, that declare what I already have. Words that say, "Jesus became poor that I may have wealth. Health is mine. The names of God are mine. The blessings come upon me and overtake me." Words that say, "I have supernatural favor! Success is mine." Words that declare the greatest of my inheritance, that I have life and life more abundantly. These are the words of grace. These words will produce what you already have in seed form. All the promises are yes and amen in Christ Jesus. (2 Corinthians 1:20)

Grace words create the environment around you. This teaching has changed my whole life. I love this scripture.

¹⁶May our Lord Jesus Christ Himself and God our Father, Who loved us and by His grace gave us eternal encouragement and good hope, ¹⁷encourage your hearts and strengthen you in every good deed and word. (2 Thessalonians 2:16-17 NIV)

Testimony

This scripture is one of those landmark scriptures in my life. It came at a time when I didn't have the revelation of grace, a time when I was in a terrible storm. God gave me this scripture, and it was the starter to bring me to the place of receiving a revelation of grace that changed me from being law driven (an earner) to a receiver of Christ's works, grace.

As I began meditating on His grace that gives us eternal encouragement and good hope, I received grace's eternal encouragement and hope to encourage my heart and strengthen me to do good and to have His words. Well, one night I woke up with the fiery darts of the enemy coming at me, but they weren't able to enter my heart. They went right over my head because the power of grace had camped in my heart. Grace gave me words of success, favor, wealth, love and faith, supernatural words.

⁶Let your conversation be always full of grace, seasoned with salt, so that you may know how to answer everyone. (Colossians 4:6 NIV)

Take the limits off. Speak words that build up and words that give encouragement, words that give an inheritance. Speak words that are full of love, success, and favor over the people in your life.

I was one of those mothers who spoke words over my children. Words that said to them that they were over-the-top amazing children of great value, successful, with supernatural favor on them, full of the love of God, kind, with great personalities and on and on. I would tell them they were geniuses. When the time came for grandchildren to come along, I spoke those words over them.

One night as I was lying by one of my grandsons, who was in kindergarten at the time, he began to tell me all the capitals in each state. I honestly don't know all of them myself. Overwhelmed by his brilliance, I told him, "You are a genius!" Well, the next time we were together, my grandson told me, "Grandma, the other kids at school told me I wasn't a genius." Well, he graduated from high school as valedictorian of his class of over 800 students, and he is now in college. I called each of my grandchildren a genius. They each are brilliant in school, love God, love church and are successful in every way being highly favored and loving to all. Their parents are outstanding parents.

There is power in speaking grace words.

Take the limits off. There is power in speaking grace words in a family, in a friendship, at work. Be free and build others up with grace words.

3 By faith we understand that the universe was formed at God's command, so that what is seen was not made out of what was visible. (Hebrews 11:3 NIV)

God's powerful words created everything we see. This scripture says to you, "You were created in His likeness and image, you are connected to God. You are now creating your tomorrows; you are speaking into your own life what God has already given you. You are taking what is in the unseen, in you, and speaking it into the seen as real in your life."

In our new Covenant of Grace, the covenant based on what Christ has already done and us receiving the works of Christ, we are called to a life of the Holy Spirit.

16So I say, walk by the Spirit, and you will not gratify the desires of the flesh. (Galatians 5:16 NIV)

When we are Holy-Spirit led, we will not gratify or fulfill, indulge or satisfy the desires, which are the appetites, addictions or cravings of the flesh. The gratifying of the flesh is so strong in the natural that it's only through the power of grace that we get free. This is the freedom that Christ in the New Covenant provided for us.

Testimony

The Holy Spirit is in me to tell me which way to go in God and fill me with His love, His victory and His freedom. As I was meditating on this truth, it took me back to remembering when the behavior of people could hurt me or make me feel rejected, but in grace, I see things differently. I can let people be who they are, not taking it personally, but staying in God's love and grace for them. I have mercy and under-standing and I'm ok with their choices. (I'm not talking about sin just every-day life itself.) It's called freedom from self.

When I was in nurses' training, we would have our studies in the morning and then go to the hospitals in the afternoon to work. We weren't allowed to work on the addictive floor because the young nurses were running away with the men who had addictive personalities on that floor.

Let's talk about this. The strongest part of the soul that God has given us is our will. We can choose heaven or hell.

We have freedom of choice. But when there are addictions involved, you can will to quit, but when the emotion of desire or appetite for the addiction arises in us, the addiction will win.

Now our will gets us to heaven when we choose Jesus, but our addiction will keep us in prison. When you are in the Spirit of God, you will get totally free of the things that hold you in captivity.

[11]*For the grace of God has appeared that offers salvation to all people. [12]It teaches us to say "No" to ungodliness and worldly passions, and to live self-controlled, upright and godly lives in this present age.* (Titus 2:11-12 NIV)

Grace has a voice that mentors and teaches us as it gives us the power and ability for total freedom from the addiction.

Testimony

I know in my own life when I received Jesus as my Lord and Savior, the Holy Spirit said to me, "You will never smoke again." (I was a smoker.) I was instantly set free!

Now my husband quit smoking on his own, but was never free of its desire, though He never smoked again, until one day he realized that he couldn't set himself free, and he gave it to God. Grace totally set him free! Grace set my husband free from the cravings for cigarettes.

[16]*As you yield freely and fully to the dynamic life and power of the Holy Spirit, you will abandon the cravings of your self-life.* (Galatians 5:16 TPT)

I want you to see this. When we yield freely and totally to the life and power of the Holy Spirit, the life of grace, then we will be able to totally give up the cravings (the longings and wants) of our self-life (the compulsions of selfishness)

17 So then, the two incompatible and conflicting forces within you are your self-life of the flesh and the new creation life of the Spirit. (Galatians 5:17 NIV)

This verse is saying that the Holy Spirit defeats those cravings of the self-life. Wow! The old self is gone when you receive Christ Jesus, but it doesn't mean that you are free of the garbage that the old self left behind. Those appetites and addictions are still there, and the Holy Spirit is the only One Who defeats those cravings.

The Holy Spirit defeats those cravings of the self-life. Wow!

17And the Holy Spirit's intense cravings hinder your old self-life from dominating you! The Holy Spirit is the only One Who defeats the cravings of your natural life. (Galatians 5:17 TPT)

Paul, by inspiration of the Holy Spirit, is telling us the how to's of being free.

18But when you are brought into the full freedom of the Spirit of Grace, you will no longer be living under the domination of the law, but soaring above it! (Galatians 5:18 TPT)

When we give ourselves totally to the life of grace, we will soar above our cravings and addictions, our self-life. Jesus set us totally free because Christ already took our old self-life to the cross and defeated it with its appetites and wants. These are the acts of the self-life and they are obvious.

19The cravings of the self-life are obvious: Sexual immorality, lustful thoughts, pornography, 20chasing after *things instead of God, manipulating others, hatred of those who get in your way, senseless arguments, resentment when others are favored, temper tantrums, angry quarrels, only thinking of yourself, being in love with your own opinions, ²¹being envious of the blessings of others, murder, uncontrolled addictions, wild parties, and all other similar behavior.* (Galatians 5:19-21 TPT)

Paul goes on to tell us what our new life offers us.

²²⁻²³*But the fruit produced by the Holy Spirit within you is divine love in all its varied expressions: joy that overflows, peace that subdues, patience that endures, kindness in action, a life full of virtue, faith that prevails, gentleness of heart, and strength of spirit. Never set the law above these qualities, for they are meant to be limitless.* (Galatians 5:22-23 TPT)

I love this translation! *Divine love*, this is God's unconditional love with all its *varied expressions*. I see it as we are giving love the way the person needs it, and there are many facets to it. Love is not love until we give it away. God's love has many different faces; the face that overflows with joy to others, joy unspeakable and full of glory, no matter what is going on. It's unconditional joy.

The life of grace causes me to soar above the circumstances so that I'm in the peace of God that makes no sense. I'm able to count it all joy, for I know I have won. I'm more that a conqueror!

The patience of God in us endures until we see the victory in the natural. We inherit the promises through faith and patience. These are all supernatural behaviors of God that rule our life and bring forth the divine nature of God. This fruit that dwells in us is able to transform us to the behavior we need at the moment. Praise God!! These qualities have no limits to them because God is a limitless God. So the more you surrender to the fruit of the Holy Spirit to flow through your life, the more the fruit grows in you. There is no limit to this.

We seem to always soar above every situation!

We were ministering at a church, and the pastor and his wife were sharing with us that years ago they began to listen to us on tape, (tapes at that time) and it literally saved their lives in Christianity. They went on to say to us, "You seem to always soar above every situation!" Well, we soar because of grace not because of us.

²³*Against such things there is no law.* (Galatians 5:23 NIV)

Grace has the power and ability to keep us, not the law. Remember, in grace, it's what Christ has done, and we bind ourselves to His works. Under law, it's what we do.

²⁴*Those who belong to Christ Jesus have crucified the flesh with its passions and desires.* (Galatians 5:24 NIV)

Oh my Goodness!! This was a life-changing scripture for me. Years ago that scripture jumped out at me, and I said, "Yes! I take those passions and desires of the flesh and see them crucified with Christ Jesus, powerless over my life, dead and buried."

This prayer totally sets you free. Then you are resurrected in the newness of life.

Grace is not a license to sin, to be selfish and hateful. Grace is not me, myself and I. In grace you are free to be others' conscious. You are serving others in love, and you soar above the things that used to feed your appetite of self. Grace makes you free from the prison of emptiness.

[25]We must live in the Holy Spirit and follow after Him. (Galatians 5:25 TPT)

In grace, we realize that by the Holy Spirit we are one-of-a-kind, unique, so we don't compare ourselves to others. We forsake all jealousy. We honor one another.

[26]So may we never be arrogant, or look down on another, for each of us is an original. We must forsake all jealousy that diminishes the value of others. (Galatians 5:26 TPT)

Grace Shows Mercy
Chapter 12

Paul, by the inspiration of the Holy Spirit, is revealing to us what the grace life should look like. God is a God of mercy so in the life of grace, we are called to show mercy. God is merciful to the merciful.

[1]*My beloved friends, if you see a believer who is overtaken with a fault, may the one who overflows with the Spirit seek to restore him. Win him over with gentle words, which will open his heart to you and will keep you from exalting yourself over him.* (Galatians 6:1 TPT)

Where God is saying, "...*overtaken with a fault...*" it can be a decision that was made that was an emotional decision and not a God decision. This decision can be something very minor or something very huge, a decision that can take us from the place of victory into disaster. God doesn't demand perfection because we are imperfect beings, but God has a great plan of redemption for us in those times.

We need to make the choice, "Do I want to be a part of the plan to work with God to restore the person?" This is an act of grace and love.

Testimony

I knew of someone who had made an emotional decision and married the wrong person, and it absolutely didn't work out. His parents were pastors. They used words of hope, eternal encouragement, love, restoration and gentleness that were able to open their son's heart. He was able to get free of the shame, condemnation, and failure and could see that God had destiny, life and life more abundantly still waiting for him. What a victory!! This is the power of our new Covenant of Grace.

Today this pastor's son is remarried with a great family of six children, has a large church and travels the world building God's Kingdom in God's love and grace. He has a voice of restoration for God's people. God's grace turns all things into good.

[1]*...may the one who overflows with the Spirit seek to restore him.* (Galatians 6:1 TPT)

The word *restore* means to *reset a dislocated bone.* Restore is a medical term. This word is a verb in the present action which says, "It might take some time." God is speaking to us and the person we are restoring into the fellowship, not to get discouraged if it doesn't happen overnight.

God doesn't expect perfection, and we need to stop that.

There are times we will make a bad decision with our finances, people, on-the-job, etc. We could have a relapse in an addiction because of discouragement or tragedy in the family, a bad doctor's report and so on. Romans Four in the Amplified Bible talks about the man who is happy, blessed and to be envied because he knows God doesn't hold his sins or faults against him or remember them anymore.

God doesn't expect perfection, and we need to stop that. Jesus is the only perfect One, and we are now joined to His perfection, not ours.

28And we know that in all things God works for the good of those who love Him, who have been called according to His purpose. (Romans 8:28 NIV)

Give it to God, and He will make it even better in His hands. God is a restorer, a redeemer, a miracle-God in the midst of our failures. We need to stop believing for bad when we blow it, and let God take our mess and redeem it, making it even greater. You get what you believe for.

Testimony

This was a turning point for me. I was demanding perfection from myself, and if I missed the mark...oh, my goodness! I believed that I had to pay big time. What a transformation in grace when God showed me that I was believing for the wrong thing. God is a restorer and redeemer not an accuser waiting to get us when we blow it. I'm free, free today of that religious lie! I love the Covenant of Grace. I'm so depending on Who Jesus is to have dominion in me.

10I make known the end from the beginning, from ancient times, what is still to come. I say, "My purpose will stand, and I will do all that I please." (Isaiah 46:10 NIV)

God knows the end from the beginning. God is saying to us, "Maybe you made a bad decision in your life...BUT GOD!" You messed up big time in some area of your life, but God is saying to you, "My purpose for you, your destiny, will stand!" Why? Because God already knows you were going to blow it, and He has a backup plan called redemption. Just embrace God's plan, and His power has already turned it into good, and He has already done it. He does all that He pleases.

God's purpose in our lives doesn't change because we are not perfect people, only Christ was perfect. This is grace.

Restore is also a picture of a dislocated bone. I had a family member who did one of those things you should never do. She climbed up high on a ladder and fell off, and she dislocated her shoulder. It was extremely painful. They treated it with gentleness and gave it all the time the shoulder needed to be healed and restored. This is the picture God wants us to grasp. We are to restore by the power of the Holy Spirit with love, tenderness and patience, using words of love, hope and encouragement, words that produce patience and faith for the person. We are to help our brother and sister to get to the top again.

8This superabundant grace is already powerfully working in us releasing within us all forms of wisdom and practical understanding. (Ephesians 1:8 TPT)

This superabundant grace is already powerfully working in us...

This superabundant grace worked in Jesus for us. Jesus healed the sick, opened blind eyes, restored the woman caught in adultery, loved and restored the woman at the well, but the legalist used those times in peoples' lives to condemn, shame and put guilt on them. Now, we hate sin, but we love the sinner.

God calls us to walk in mercy, not to complain about the weak person, gossip, treat them roughly or run them out of fellowship, but to gently put them in the right place in the Body. We have to understand that it will take time for them to function correctly again. We need to give them love, patience, and the time they need to grow strong so they can slowly take on the responsibility that belongs to them.

The legalist condemns this person, but the Spirit-led person restores them. Religion shoots the wounded or kicks them when they are down. They condemn, shame and make them feel guilty, but what God is saying is, "Be loving, merciful, show brotherly kindness and be humble in spirit toward them."

We should never doubt the power of grace to restore no matter how big the problem is. In grace, we never use words of condemnation, guilt or judgement. When we use grace words, it will cause the person's heart to be open to us and keep us from entering into pride.

God has called us to be people of love. The new commandment Jesus gave us is to love one another as Jesus loved us. (John 13:34) The Bible says grace gives us good words, words filled with eternal encouragement and hope. Grace gives us the ministry of restoration. In grace, our ministry is restoring people to their place in God's Kingdom and saving a multitude of people.

When we look at Jesus as He walked on this earth, He did not have a ministry of condemnation, guilt, judgement or shame, but one of love and restoration. We now need to step into the ministry of Christ. It's Christ in me, the hope of glory. (Colossians 1:27 NIV) I need to depend on Christ to flow through me.

The Word of God says no man can tame the tongue, (James 3:8) but, in Christ Jesus, I have been given His tongue which is the sword of the Spirit. Grace has given me the words of Christ.

12For the Word of God is alive and active. Sharper than any double-edged sword, it penetrates even to dividing soul and spirit, joints and marrow; it judges the thoughts and attitudes of the heart. (Hebrews 4:12 NIV)

[16]*...and coming out of His* (Jesus) *mouth was a sharp, double-edged sword.* (Revelation 1:16 NIV)

Christ was a restorer when He walked this earth. Christ has given us a picture of how grace, the New Covenant, should look.

[18]*All this is from God, Who reconciled us to Himself through Christ and gave us the ministry of reconciliation:* [19]*that God was reconciling the world to Himself in Christ, not counting people's sins against them. And He has committed to us the message of reconciliation.* (2 Corinthians 5:18-19 NIV)

[27]*When Jesus stepped ashore, He was met by a demon-possessed man from the town. For a long time this man had not worn clothes or lived in a house, but had lived in the tombs.* [28]*When he saw Jesus, he cried out and fell at His feet, shouting at the top of his voice,*

"What do you want with me, Jesus, Son of the Most High God? I beg you, don't torture me!"

[29]*For Jesus had commanded the impure spirit to come out of the man. Many times it had seized him, and though he was chained hand and foot and kept under guard, he had broken his chains and had been driven by the demon into solitary places.* [30]*Jesus asked him,*

"What is your name?"

"Legion," He replied, because many demons had gone into him. [31]*And they begged Jesus repeatedly not to order them to go into the Abyss.* [32]*A large herd of pigs was feeding there on the hillside. The demons begged Jesus to let them go into the pigs, and He gave them permission.* [33]*When the demons came out of the man, they went into the pigs, and the herd rushed down the steep bank into the lake and was drowned.*

³⁴When those tending the pigs saw what had happened, they ran off and reported this in the town and countryside, ³⁵and the people went out to see what had happened. When they came to Jesus, they found the man from whom the demons had gone out, sitting at Jesus' feet, dressed and in his right mind; and they were afraid. ³⁶Those who had seen it told the people how the demon-possessed man had been cured. (Luke 8:27-36 NIV)

The man in the region of the Gerasenes caused a lot of harm to the city. Jesus didn't condemn, shame or judge him, but restored him with love and compassion. This is how grace should look in our lives.

Jesus didn't condemn, shame or judge him,
but restored him with love and compassion.

---

²Love empowers us to fulfill the law of the Anointed One as we carry each other's troubles. (Galatians 6:2 TPT)

The law of the Anointed One (Christ) is a New Covenant of love. The legalists in Jesus' day did the opposite of restoring. They heaped heavy burdens upon the people by using these moments to abuse, shame, condemn, use guilt and stone them to death.

⁴They tie up heavy, cumbersome loads and put them on other people's shoulders, but they themselves are not willing to lift a finger to move them. (Matthew 23:4 NIV)

Many times it's just the words we say or how we say it. Peter intercedes on behalf of the Gentile Christians. He asked the Jewish Christian leaders not to put heavy burdens on the people of God in the Covenant of Grace.

10Now then, why do you try to test God by putting on the necks of Gentiles a yoke that neither we nor our ancestors have been able to bear? (Acts 15:10 NIV)

God can reveal to us the legalism in our hearts about a brother or sister in God's Kingdom who missed the mark. If our hearts are filled with judgement and condemnation towards them, along with pride, we have to be honest with ourselves, and see it nailed to the cross and be free from that attitude.

20Never doubt God's mighty power to work in you and accomplish all this. He will achieve infinitely more than your greatest request, your most unbelievable dream, and exceed your wildest imagination! He will outdo them all, for His miraculous power constantly energizes you. (Ephesians 3:20 TPT)

The Word says never doubt the power in grace, and grace fuels the passion of love in our hearts.

9My passion is to enlighten every person to this divine mystery. (Ephesians 3:9 TPT)

6But He gives us more grace. That is why Scripture says: "God opposes the proud but gives grace to the humble." (James 4:6 NIV84)

The humbleness in grace is Christ in us, and the Holy Spirit giving us the right words to say, not our words but His words. The Holy Spirit gives us the words to get them back into their position, in the Body of Christ, restored by the supernatural power of God.

3For if anyone thinks himself to be something, when he is nothing, he deceives himself. (Galatians 6:3 NKJ)

The deception that Paul is talking about here is that of self-importance without Christ. Christ is the Head, and the life flows from the Head, and we can do nothing without Christ.

Though I'm in the family of God, Christ in me, the hope of glory, Paul is pointing out, that we can be tempted to think, "I'm so great! Of course I can help him. Let me at him!" We're not realizing it's the Holy Spirit Who gives us the right words.

⁵I am the vine; you are the branches. If you remain in Me and I in you, you will bear much fruit; apart from Me you can do nothing. (John 15:5 NIV)

Your adequacy comes from God.

⁴Such confidence we have through Christ before God. ⁵Not that we are competent in ourselves to claim anything for ourselves, but our competence comes from God. ⁶He has made us competent as ministers of a new covenant—not of the letter but of the Spirit; for the letter kills, but the Spirit gives life. (2 Corinthians 3:4-6 NIV)

God has called us to the life of the Spirit.

¹³And I find that the strength of Christ's explosive power infuses me to conquer every difficulty. (Philippians 4:13 TPT)

⁵For each one shall bear his own load. (Galatians 6:5 NKJ)

I used to be confused by this scripture because Galatians 6:2 says, *"carry each other's burdens..."* Help them through it. This verse seems to imply to carry their load until they get on their feet, and verse five says, *"each one should carry their own load."* And I would think, "Well, which one is it? Carry or don't carry?" Well, in Galatians 6:5, this is talking about responsibility. The Greek word in Galatians 6:4 for burden is *phortion* which means, *something to be carried* (our responsibilities, obligations, calling).

In verse five, *burden* is the same word that's used in association with carrying a soldier's pack. A soldier carries his own pack and is not to expect another to carry it. Each bears the responsibility for his own pack.

We each have our own lane, our own race, our own destiny to run. We have responsibilities and obligations in that race to fulfill or receive what Christ already fulfilled, and let it flow through us. So you have the grace to do it. Jesus' yoke is easy and His burden is light. (Matthew 11:30 NIV)

God wants you to discern when someone
has been victimized or if someone is a victim in life.

What this scripture in Galatians is saying is that there will be people who will want you to run their race, to take on their responsibility, and carry their destiny, but the Holy Spirit is saying not to do this. God has called you to receive your race, your destiny, not someone else's. God wants you to discern when someone has been victimized or if someone is a victim in life.

Victims in life are those who are addicted to self. They are extremely self-centered. Their whole thought process is, "How can I get you to take care of me, run my race, carry my load, and take on my obligations and responsibilities." This is their drug. It is self, and they get a high when you do carry their load. They feel loved. They have no plans to ever get better, but they will act like they are trying if they feel you are tiring of taking care of them.

In this addiction to self, they have an inability to think beyond themselves and their needs. Their tools, to get you to carry their load, are through guilt, shame and condemnation. They escalate to the highest degree to get you to take care of them even at the expense of your own family or destiny. Life is all about them, and they put themselves above God. The enemy brings them into your life to steal your destiny. They are first-fruit stealers in the Kingdom.

The worst thing we can do is pick up their load because then we don't allow them get free of their self-centeredness. We need to let them come to the end of themselves, to make a decision to hate this life behavior, to hate the world of self-centeredness, to want to carry their own load, and to get free of the addiction of self, the victim role.

Testimony

I understand this world because I was the enabler to the victim. I was raised in a dysfunctional family, and I became the enabler of the family. When I entered into my Christian life, I took that role with me. I would start to run my race, take on my destiny, and then a victim would show up in my life. I would be totally into carrying their load. The Holy Spirit began to work with me about my problem of being addicted to being an enabler. You see an enabler gets their high from taking care of a victim. They feel like the hero, that person's savior.

I was, at this stage of my life, surrounded by victims. My husband and I were called of God to start a church. The Holy Spirit was faithful to begin the process of revealing to my husband and me our addiction of carrying the victim's load. We tried to get free with our own strength and decision but failed miserably. By the leading of the Holy Spirit, we went on a four-day fast. After four days, I had an open vision, and the Holy Spirit revealed to me, that when I entered into taking care of a victim, I got off God's path for me and was beside the path but not on it. We repented and were totally set free!

You have to understand that person, playing the role of the victim, has the anointing, the ability to run their own race and you don't. God already fulfilled their destiny in His heart for them. When you try to pick up someone else's race, you don't have the anointing or the power to run it. It will just steal your destiny, your time, your family and even your race.

When you try to pick up someone else's race,
you don't have the anointing or the power to run it.

God wants us to love the person but hate the behavior because it's stealing destiny from the victim. How do we help them? We need to speak truth in love. This is an addiction in their life. God has an amazing life for them, and this is stealing it from them. This behavior is not a blessing, and they need to hate it. In grace, God has already fulfilled their destiny in His heart for them, and they need to receive it.

[11]*Before we were even born, He gave us our destiny; that we would fulfill the plan of God Who always accomplishes every purpose and plan in His heart.* (Ephesians 1:11 TPT)

God set them up as a winner. Offer them prayer for freedom from the victim realm, but do not pick up their load. Give them an assignment of reading God's Word, quoting scriptures, listening to faith and grace teachings, coming to church to sit under God's Word and entering into worship.

[2]*And do not be conformed to this world, but be transformed by the renewing of your mind, that you may prove what is that good and acceptable and perfect will of God.* (Romans 12:2 NKJ)

168

They need a new thought pattern.

[8]Finally, brethren, whatever things are true, whatever things are noble, whatever things are just, whatever things are pure, whatever things are lovely, whatever things are of good report, if there is any virtue and if there is anything praiseworthy—meditate on these things. (Philippians 4:8 NKJ)

Don't let them steal your destiny. Recognize when they are using condemnation, guilt and shame on you. Meet with them only if they are doing these things and the Holy Spirit is saying yes.

For a more thorough understanding of the victim and enabler personalities, please read my book, *Name of the Game of Life, Victim, Enabler, Persecutor, Helper.*

Grace is a Life of Giving
Chapter 13

Paul, by inspiration of the Holy Spirit, is unfolding to us what grace should look like. In grace, we step into our new identity, an identity that looks like Jesus. We are a giver not a taker. We are full of love, mercy, and power. A ministry or a behavior of a giver is one who receives the works of Christ as finished and lets it flow to them to give to others.

6The one who is taught the Word [of God] is to share all good things with his teacher [contributing to his spiritual and material support]. (Galatians 6:6 AMP)

God is saying here not only to be thankful and appreciative for those who have contributed to our spiritual needs, but to also show it by our financial giving.

We found in our own lives, that being in the ministry will cost you all. God is saying that your financial giving into those who have set you up to win in life by teaching you God's way, is part of grace. You can never out give God.

Your giving is God's system to walking out of poverty.

Grace is believing and receiving what God said is true about our giving. I trust God when He says, "If you give financially, it will be multiplied back to you." (Luke 6:38) Your giving is God's system to walking out of poverty. Grace is not about you, but about others. In grace, you died to self.

10...Yes, this was written for us, because whoever plows and threshes should be able to do so in the hope of sharing in the harvest. 11If we have sown spiritual seed among you, is it too much if we reap a material harvest from you? 14In the same

170

way, the Lord has commanded that those who preach the Gospel should receive their living from the Gospel. (I Corinthians 9:10, 11, 14 NIV)

God's Kingdom is about giving. It's never a one-way street. Think about this. A farmer plants a seed in the natural, and there will be a thousand seeds from that seed. Well, in the Kingdom of God, when you plant a financial seed, there is a supernatural multiplication on that seed. See, the natural realm is a picture to us of what happens in the unseen in God's Kingdom. Understanding Kingdom principles, we need to give out of our need to break out of poverty, to get a raise, to go to the next level in our finances.

Testimony

I remember one time in my husband and my life when we were opened to supernatural giving by the Holy Spirit. We began to pray about giving supernaturally. (This means giving all your finances.) At that time, we were getting a set wage every two weeks. So twice, my husband gave it all into the ministry. Now at that time, we had an average income. We were a middle-class family financially.

By our supernatural giving, the floodgates of heaven were opened to us. We went from an average-income family to millionaires. Every door of wealth seemed to be supernaturally opened to us. It was a little overwhelming at times. The floodgates were opened. I can tell you from our experience, it works!

Now, it is important in the ministry that we aren't trying to get money from you, but we are trying to get money to you.

[17]Not that I desire your gifts; what I desire is that more be credited to your account. (Philippians 4:17 NIV)

As a leader, we have to have the right motive. It can't be about the leader. It must be about the people.

[17]Not that I seek the gift itself, but I do seek the profit which increases to your [heavenly] account [the blessing which is accumulating for you]. [18]But I have received everything in full and more; I am amply supplied, having received from Epaphroditus the gifts you sent me. They are the fragrant aroma of an offering, an acceptable sacrifice which God welcomes and in which He delights. (Philippians 4:17-18 AMP)

One translation says that your harvest of blessings will increase.

[19]And my God will meet all your needs according to the riches of His glory in Christ Jesus. (Philippians 4:19 NIV)

Think about this. A farmer gets his field ready to plant seed, decides not to plant the seed, but he still believes he is going to have a harvest. We would think the farmer is acting foolishly, but how many times do we do that very thing? We get the soil of our hearts ready for seed, and then we don't plant financial seed, but we are expecting a financial harvest.

[7]Make no mistake about it, God will never be mocked! For what you plant will be the very thing you harvest. (Galatians 6:7 TPT)

[7]Do not be deceived, God is not mocked [He will not allow Himself to be ridiculed, nor treated with contempt nor allow His precepts to be scornfully set aside]; for whatever a man sows, this and this only is what he will reap. (Galatians 6:7 AMP)

Many people want to do a lot of reaping financially but never do any sowing.

6Remember this: Whoever sows sparingly will also reap sparingly, and whoever sows generously will also reap generously. (2 Corinthians 9:6 NIV)

6Now [remember] this: he who sows sparingly will also reap sparingly, and he who sows generously [that blessings may come to others] will also reap generously [and be blessed]. (2 Corinthians 9:6 AMP)

When you step into the life of grace, you step into the life of giving. God so loved that He gave. (John 3:16) Jesus gave it all. When we step into grace, we are the image of the invisible God. God wants an awareness of increase in your life, and this is the reason you are to share your goods. When you sow financially into the Kingdom of God, you are sowing so others can be blessed. This is the life of grace. It's you having a heart to cover the earth with God's Word to reach those who are in a legalistic prison, those under religion, those who need salvation, etc.

God wants an awareness of increase in your life, and this is the reason you are to share your goods.

I looked up the meaning of the word *generously,* (*...he who sows generously...* 2 Cor. 9:6) and it means: abundantly, reap bountifully, too much, inexhaustible blessings. God is saying, "Get rid of that poverty thinking, that greed, that withholding way of life."

24One person gives freely, yet gains even more; another withholds unduly, but comes to poverty. 25A generous person will prosper; whoever refreshes others will be refreshed. (Proverbs 11:24-25 NIV)

Growing up, in the town I lived in, I knew someone who was a workaholic. He never took a day off. He was very anti-church, and said, "They just want your money." He was planning his retirement, so he took all of his capital gain and invested it all. He mortgaged everything he had to financially set himself up for the rest of his life. However, that year everything collapsed, and he lost everything. If we steal from God, the devil has a right to steal from us.

⁸The harvest you reap reveals the seed that was planted. If you plant the corrupt seeds of self-life into this natural realm, you can expect to experience a harvest of corruption. If you plant the good seeds of Spirit-life you will reap the beautiful fruits that grow from the everlasting life of the Spirit. (Galatians 6:8 TPT)

⁸The person who plants selfishness, ignoring the needs of others – ignoring God! – harvests a crop of weeds. All he'll have to show for his life is weeds! But the one who plants in response to God, letting God's Spirit do the growth work in him, harvests a crop of real life, eternal life. (Galatians 6:8 MSG)

⁸For he who sows to his flesh will out of the flesh reap corruption, but he who sows to the Spirit will of the Spirit reap everlasting life. (Galatians 6:8 NKJ)

The Message Bible says sowing your finances to yourself is sowing weeds. It will not produce good things for you. The New King James says you will reap corruption. We know in the natural that weeds choke out the good seed.

What is God saying here? When you sow financially into the Kingdom of God, you will reap the blessings. Now you already have the blessings in God's Kingdom. They are yours, and this is God's way of releasing them to you.

Now, in your sowing of finances, be patient. When a farmer plants his seed, he knows it's going to take time for the harvest. Again, in the spiritual realm, we need to know when we plant our financial seed, it is going to take time before we see the harvest. So you must be patient.

Now you already have the blessings in God's Kingdom.
They are yours, and this is God's way of releasing them to you.

---

⁹And don't allow yourselves to be weary or dis-heartened in planting good seeds, for the season of reaping the wonderful harvest you've planted is coming! (Galatians 6:9 TPT)

God promised you a harvest, and God doesn't lie. In this scripture, God warns us about growing weary. So don't! Our impatience can cause us to faint and not reap our harvest.

⁹My passion is to enlighten every person to this divine mystery. (Ephesians 3:9 TPT)

⁸Grace alone empowers me. (Ephesians 3:8 TPT)

PRAYER OF SALVATION

Salvation does not mean following a bunch of rules to try to keep God happy. The truth is that He loves you and wants you to experience joy, health, peace and prosperity. You can only do that knowing Jesus as a Friend and Savior.

How can you be saved? It is a matter of simply believing. The Bible says: If you confess with your mouth the Lord Jesus and believe in your heart that God has raised Him from the dead, you will be saved. (Romans 10:9)

If you believe, then pray this prayer:
"Dear Father God, I ask you to forgive me of all my sins. Jesus, come into my heart, come into my life, be my Lord and Savior. In Jesus name, Amen. Jesus is Lord!"

Congratulations! You made the very best decision you have ever made or ever will make. Now you are saved. You are forgiven and you are on your way to heaven. The next step is to grow in this new relationship with God. The best way to do that is to read your Bible every day so that God can speak to you through it, and get involved in a good church so that you can have support and fellowship with other believers.

We would love to hear from you!
If you received Christ as your personal Savior, we want to send you a free Bible. Email us at Maureen@thewordforwinners.com or visit us online at Thewordforwinners.com

MORE BOOKS BY THE ANDERSONS

Dr. Maureen Anderson (See thewordforwinners.com)
Releasing the Miraculous Through Fasting with Prayer
Are You Spirit Led or Emotionally Driven
Damaged DNA
Making Impossibilities Possible
Confessing God's Word (Leather Bound)
Open the Door to Your Miracle

Drs. C. Thomas and Maureen Anderson
Marriage Beyond the Dream
Name of the Game-Victim, Enabler, Persecutor, Helper
Health God's Way

Dr. C. Thomas Anderson (See drcthomasanderson.org)
Becoming a Millionaire God's Way Part 1
Becoming a Millionaire God's Way Part 2
Will the Real America Please Stand Up?
No More Sacred Cows, Grace > Religion
*LOL Your Way to Life – Anecdotes and One-Liners to Get You
    through Your Day*
Releasing the Blessings You Can't Contain
Intelligence by Design
*Personal Growth to Power – Jesus Between the Lines-18 Power
    Principles to Success*
The Big Six of Genesis
Grace Carved in Wood
Mind Over What Matters
The Money System, Are You Being Dumbed Down?
The Essence of Creation - 7 Principles
*Please Train Up You're Your Child - Character Determines
    Your Child's Destiny*

INVITE DR. MAUREEN ANDERSON TO SPEAK!

If you desire to have Dr. Maureen Anderson speak at your event or church, please call 1-866-253-4678 or visit our website, **thewordforwinners.com** and fill out the booking invite form or email maureen@thewordforwinners.com

Join The Word for Winners Family today!

Yes, I want to join Maureen Anderson in partnership. Enclosed is my first offering of $ _____ to establish my monthly partnership and help reach the world with the Word of Grace.

_____ Please contact me to show me how to receive my free e-book for becoming a monthly partner.

Name _____

Address _____

City _____

State _____ Zip _____

Phone (_____) _____

Email _____

_____ I would like to set up an automatic gift from my debit or credit card.

_____ I would like to donate one time today.

Card Number _____ Code _____

Expiration Date _____

Name on the Card _____

Send to: The Word for Winners
            P.O. Box 22229
            Mesa, AZ 85277

I sow this seed in faith believing that God will meet my need:_____

Thank You!
If you would like prayer, call the prayer line, 480-669-0102.
www.thewordforwinners.com